My Expectation is From Him

Infertility: Surviving it spiritually

Sarah Erb

My Expectation is From Him
Infertility: Surviving it spiritually

©2011 Copyright Erb Publishers
No part of this book may be modified without express permission from the author/publisher.

Printed in the USA by
FBC Publications & Printing
Fort Pierce, FL 34982
www.fbcpublications.com

For the many friends who are and have been with me on this journey

"That your faith should not stand in the wisdom of man, but in the power of God." 1 Corinthians 2:5

CONTENTS

Foreword: My Story   7

A Map of Infertility and Adoption in the Bible

Sarah: Hope for the Hopeless	13
Rebekah: the Power of Prayer	19
Rachel: the Regretful Response	23
Pharaoh's Daughter: Compassion to Foster	27
Samson's Mother: God is in Control	31
Hannah: A Heart for God	35
Elisabeth: God's Perfect Timing	43
Michal: Looking for Fault in Others	47
The Shunammite Woman: God's Goodness	51
Esther: A Future Designed by God	53
Jesus: In All Ways Tempted as We Are	57

The Advice You *Really* Need: Ten Spiritual Counsels from Those who have been there

Pray Without Ceasing: God as a Resting Place	63
Read God's Word and Apply It: God as a Buckler	67
Choose the Right Attitude: God as a Whirlwind	71
Manifest God Through Your Struggle: God as an Ointment	75
Accept Other Alternatives: God as a Redeemer	79
Don't Give in or Give Up: God as a Rock	83
Reach Out to Others: God as a Vine	87
Wait For Now, Not Tomorrow: God as a Craftsman	91

Don't Let in Bitterness: God as a Mountain	93
Submit to God's Will: God as a Road Map	97

Exercising the Fruits of the Spirit amidst Infertility

Love	101
Joy	103
Peace	105
Longsuffering	107
Gentleness	109
Goodness	111
Faith	113
Meekness	115
Temperance	117
Afterword: Motherhood after Infertility	121

Foreword

"He maketh the barren woman to be a keeper at home and a joyful mother of children..."(Psalm 113:9)

If you had asked me at the beginning of 2006 to describe what I thought God had in store for my husband and me; I never would have proclaimed this verse. In fact, in my darkest moments, I had envisioned my life as empty and barren as my womb had been for the previous four years. Our struggle with infertility had both encompassed us in a battle for our spiritual well-being and empowered us with the strength to face another day of hope-filled longing for a child. At the same time I watched, and still do, as many who share our struggle succumb to the bitterness and depression that infertility can bring. Others lean on Christ and rise above the sinking weight that Satan tries to use to destroy them. It truly is a roller coaster of emotions. I rejoice that God gave us the strength through His Word as well as the Godly advice of Christian friends who were familiar with our struggle. The purpose of this book is to share with you, dear reader, that this strength can be yours as well.

After a long period of dating, my husband and I were married in May of 2002. We were looking forward to adding to our family, but we felt it would be best to wait about a year before we started trying to conceive. I could not wait to become pregnant. After our year had passed and we were officially "trying", I began to feel very unsettled and feared that I would not be able to get pregnant. I talked with my doctor, who did not seem too concerned. After another year had passed, he officially diagnosed us with unexplained infertility. He ran all the typical tests to try to pinpoint the problem, but nothing could be found. There were no apparent physical problems with either my husband or me. For many, including myself, this is a terribly disconcerting feeling. You are unable to do what the general population takes for granted; something is wrong, but no one can tell you what. At the same time it is such a private struggle and often filled with unwanted or unrequested advice from everyone, even perfect strangers.

The last step in our testing phase was for me to have a laparoscopy to look for blockage in my fallopian tubes or endometriosis. I was unsure if I really wanted to undergo surgery, even though it was minor, because my husband and I were at peace with the calling of God to adopt a child. A friend of mine who had been through infertility at a younger age, advised me to go through with the laparoscopy and HSG (Hysterosalpingogram) for my own peace of mind. In April of 2006, I underwent the laparoscopy which revealed a 100% blockage of my right fallopian tube. In fact it was knotted so badly, the doctor could not fix it and informed me that my best option was to go through another surgery to have it removed in hopes of the other tube taking over. For the most part, this explained our infertility, but I still had one tube that was fully functional. It also presented the danger of a tubal pregnancy. I decided to forgo another surgery and wait it out.

At the beginning of 2006, we began the process to get our foster care license. We wanted to adopt, but it is such an expensive and time consuming process. We felt that we could help more children in the meantime by fostering infants in hopes of one coming up for adoption. We knew this might be a very painful and difficult task, but we felt it was what God wanted us to do. We attended our first training at the local Department of Human Services and were excited at the prospect of bringing children into our home soon.

In April of 2006, we were approached by a young woman who was about seven months pregnant and was going to give the baby up for adoption. We talked with her and thought that it would be best that she get some counseling about her situation. We went to a local agency that provided counseling services as well as facilitating private adoptions. We began the paperwork to complete the home study and other requirements for the adoption process. After about a month, however, the birth mother changed her mind and decided to parent the child. This was a painful turn of events for us, but we felt as if we should continue pursuing foster care--only with this new agency instead of the original Department of Human Services.

As we began the process of becoming licensed for foster care, we found out that a teenager who was part of our youth program at church was entering the foster care system. She had been in trouble and in the juvenile system for some time; this was her last resort. Her probation officer found out we were becoming foster parents and asked us if we would consider helping her. We prayed about it and, though we were prepared to take infants, we said yes.

This was the beginning of our journey. While I realize everybody's journey will not end the same way, it is my hope that the advice and biblical truths in this book will encourage someone on this journey, or help someone to understand what this experience is like. If you are going through infertility right now, please know that the things said in this book are not meant to make you feel as though you are doing something wrong or that there is some way that you can 'earn' children by getting spiritual help. In the sensitive emotional state you are in, please know that the things I write are truthful and intended to help good growth come out of a trying circumstance regardless of its outcome.

A Map of Infertility and Adoption throughout the Bible

Chapter 1
Sarah, Hope for the hopeless

"Now Sarai Abram's wife bare him no children..."
Genesis 16:1

"And he brought him forth abroad, and said, LOOK NOW TOWARD HEAVEN, AND TELL THE STARS, IF THOU BE ABLE TO NUMBER THEM: and he said unto him, SO SHALL THY SEED BE." Genesis 15:5

The doors opened and I was greeted by friendly smiles and handshakes. But the stairs loomed in front of me like the jagged edge of a rocky peak and I was the mountain climber. I could not give up now, it was too late. The crowd in front of me parted like wild stag veering from some viscous predator and there she was. Crouched low and ready to spring on the weakest prey. I found myself alone; the rest of the herd fleeing from the attack. "So," she said with far more excitement than necessary. "Guess what today is?" As if I didn't know; I knew all too well. The temptation to stay home on this day was so strong that I had almost come down with a case of the flu. Mother's Day: The day that all those who are experiencing infertility dread. It would be a day of questions--"when are you going to be a mother?"; a day of embarrassment-- "will all those who are mothers please stand and be recognized"; and a day of pain-- "today I want to preach on the story of Abraham and Sarah, and how their faith allowed God to bless them with a child".

    One of the most commonly known stories about infertility in the Bible is the story of Abraham and Sarah. It is also one that many experiencing infertility find difficult to digest. Most individuals who are trying to conceive are not past childbearing age, and God has never spoken to them from heaven to promise that they will someday have children. When this is preached in churches, it is most often told as a story of faith and we can sometimes feel as if we do not have enough faith because God has not blessed us with a child. I even heard a well-meaning preacher say once that people who cannot have children should have more faith. He said that they should go and decorate a room in their house as a nursery in preparation of God's blessing. Little did he know that my husband and I had a nursery that had been decorated for two years. It is hard to find hope in a world where it seems as if everyone around you has no idea how it feels to be childless and longing for a child. Most people assume that if you do not have children, it is by choice and they feel the need to ask you when you are going to start trying. While the story of Abraham and Sarah *is* a story of great faith and of how God blessed his faithful servants, this is not where our hope is to be found. Sarai herself even laughed at God's plan to bless her with a child "when she was past age". The greatest hope to be found in the story of Abraham and Sarah is not in their ability to eventually have a child, but in God's ability to keep His promises and the strength they found along the way.

"Through faith also Sara herself received strength to

conceive seed, and was delivered of a child when she was past age, because she judged him faithful who had promised." Hebrews 11:11

The Bible says a great deal about the promises of God. It also says a lot about hope. And if there is one thing that people experiencing infertility need, it is hope. The Bible says in Proverbs 13:12 *"Hope deferred maketh the heart sick; but when the desire cometh, it is a tree of life."* When the hope of having a child is deferred by infertility, it can make us spiritually and emotionally, sometimes even physically sick. On days when the reminder of our 'hope deferred' is even stronger, such as Mother's Day, we need to lean on the promises of God to renew our hope and give our spirit new life. In the midst of infertility it can seem as if hope is nowhere to be found. But God specializes in seemingly hopeless situations. In Abraham's case, it even says that *"...against hope [Abraham] believed in hope, that he might become the father of many nations, according to that which was spoken, So shall thy seed be."* (Romans 4:18)

So what can we do to nourish hope in what God has planned for us? In Psalm 16:8-9 the Bible tells us: *"I have set the LORD always before me: because he is at my right hand, I shall not be moved. Therefore my heart is glad, and my glory rejoiceth: my flesh also shall rest in hope."* By keeping God at the forefront of our thoughts and the LORD Jesus Christ always by our side, we will have limitless strength. God will give us a happiness that allows us to rejoice in Him and a rest, or peace, that passes human understanding. In contrast to this, we can also suffocate hope in our life. The Bible calls it "deferring" which means "to draw away". I am pretty sure that God does not draw away from us, nor does He rob us of our ability to hope. So this tells me that as sinners, we can turn from our hope in Him and be drawn away by the lusts of this world. In Hebrews 13:5, God's word warns us, to *"be content with such things as ye have: for he hath said, I will never leave thee, nor forsake thee."* This can be a very painful truth. Yes, God wants to give us the desires of our heart, but He wants the first desire of our heart to be for Him- *"Jesus said unto him, Thou shalt love the Lord thy God with all thy heart, and with all thy soul, and with all thy mind." (Matthew 22:37)* The quickest way to lose sight of hope is to draw away from God. *"Draw nigh to God and He will draw nigh to you." (James 4:8)* If our hope is not in the Lord, it is not true hope.

So how can we apply this practically in such a negative world? Christians and non-Christians alike besiege us on a daily basis with criticism, gossip, negativity, pessimism, and thoughtlessness. It is easy to turn to these things as a crutch for our wounded spirit. Childlessness is one of those things that require a faith that just cannot be faked. If we do not learn to seek out God's solutions and truths, our pseudo-faith will flounder and we will find our self drowning in a sea of self pity and negative and bitter criticism of those around us. God's promises give us hope in a hopeless world. On difficult days when there are intrusive questions, know that God is the answer:

But know that the LORD hath set apart him that is godly for himself: the LORD will hear when I call unto him. (Psalm 4:3)

On depressing days when you feel ashamed, know

that God can lift you up:

But thou, O LORD, art a shield for me; my glory, and the lifter up of mine head. (Psalm 3:3)

On despairing days when the pain is unbearable and you want to hide, know that God can hide you:

The LORD also will be a refuge for the oppressed, a refuge in times of trouble. (Psalm 9:9)

God also tells us to lean on those He has brought into our life to help us. Perhaps you know someone in your church that has been through infertility, or you can ask your Pastor to recommend someone. Let them know what you are struggling with and allow them to pray with you and talk to you about what God taught them.

Expectant Thoughts

1. Read Hebrews 11. How many times are Abraham and/or Sarah mentioned here? How can we see hope evident in their lives through times when it seemed they had no hope? (Genesis 16).
2. How have you nourished hope through your journey so far? What can you do to allow God to guide you into His hope for your life?
3. What are some things that are hard for you to bear? Who can you turn to to be a 'burden bearer' for you? (Galatians 6:2)
4. Read through Psalm 1. What are some of God's promises to you? What are the conditions of these promises?

Chapter 2
Rebekah, The power of prayer

"And Isaac intreated the Lord for his wife, because she was barren..." Genesis 25:21

The laughter of children surrounded me as I lay buried under a pile of autumn leaves one unusually warm day in mid-November. I was not the mother of all these joyful miracles, but I was an influence in their life. As a preschool teacher for 5 years, I will admit it was difficult at times to work with other people's children and deal with infertility at the same time. I would often go home after work and feel suffocated by a job I loved, as if something completely unobtainable was within my grasp, but I could not quite make it my own. Just like hearing the laughter from under those leafs. Most days I would eat my lunch in my car in the parking lot of the elementary school. I watched people pick up their children and wondered at the way some of them were treated. I also watched those with loving relationships and cried about what I might never experience. Soon, I realized that being in tears did not make for a good finish to the rest of my day. I began to truly use this time to get closer to God. Often I begged God to reveal His will for my life. I had never been closer to God than I was in those days of prayer and fasting in my car on my lunch break. Prayer is a powerful thing. It is our lifeline to God. You see, we can wallow in the mud hole of our condition all we want, but that will only get us dirty. It is okay to feel the pain of infertility. It is real and undeniable. But God wants us to go to Him, not rely on our own fearful imaginings and worthless worry. Prayerlessness leads only to sinfulness. Isaac, the promised son of Abraham and Sarah must have learned this lesson from his parents.

    As the saga of infertility continues within this family, it is important to find God's plan for each circumstance of infertility. We must believe this for ourselves as well. This was one of the things I struggled with the most. How could God have a perfect plan for us that required us to go through so much heartache? Month after month we waited and hoped and prayed. Each month was a reminder that something within us was not working the way it was supposed to, and we had no idea what it was. We went to our pastor and he anointed us with oil as we asked God for healing and for a miracle. In our human minds, we cannot understand God's time. It is impossible for us to grasp that He is everywhere all the time and in every time. He is in complete control. We live in a fast-food society. We want our prayers answered *now*. By nature, we humans can better cope when the answer is "No," than if it is "Wait". Seeing God as a 'genie in a magic lamp' is one of the dangers of living in such an impatient world. Prayers often seem to go unanswered for periods of time before God is ready to reveal His plan. He is not ignoring us. He is simply saying "Wait.". The rest of Genesis 25:21 shows that, in Isaac's situation, the prayer *was* answered with "yes". *"...and the Lord was intreated of him, and Rebekah his wife conceived."* The Bible also makes a point of giving the age of Isaac when he and Rebekah married (Genesis 25:20), and how old he was when their children were born (Genesis 25:26). The time span between these two ages is 20 years. 20 years is a long time to wait for a prayer to be answered.

In 1 Samuel, Hannah prayed continuously for a child and her request was also granted in God's timing. We can never know when God's timing is, but we do know that God wants us to ask Him for the things we desire. *"Ask, and it shall be given you; seek, and ye shall find; knock, and it shall be opened unto you"* (Matthew 7:7) God also wants us to delight in Him; *"Delight thyself also in the LORD: and he shall give thee the desires of thine heart."* Psalm 37:4

I believe these two verses go hand in hand. God wants us to ask Him, but He also wants us to be content with what He gives us. This means that, though we may not see an instantaneous answer to our prayers, He still wants us to praise Him and be happy with what He has given us. The bible is specific that the barren womb is "never satisfied" (Proverbs 30:15-16). This does not give us permission to give up on God or to be unhappy with His other blessings in our lives.

Psalm 40 is a specific psalm about waiting on God. It says, *"I waited patiently for the LORD; and he inclined unto me, and heard my cry. He brought me up also out of an horrible pit, out of the miry clay, and set my feet upon a rock, and established my goings. And he hath put a new song in my mouth, even praise unto our God: many shall see it, and fear, and shall trust in the LORD."* (Psalm 40:1-3)

I believe that the latter half of this verse is one of the most important. The eyes of those who are not Christians are looking at us, and when we go through difficult times, they want to see what we will do. By nature, most people are skeptical about supernatural things. Some of them are just waiting for Christians to 'fail' so they can jump out and say "I told you so". This sets us up for an unfair disadvantage in the game of life. However, it does not negate our responsibility to Christ. It would be easy if God just answered all our prayers the way we wanted Him to and in our timing, but He has a divine plan for each and every one of us. The hardest part about accepting God's answers to our prayers when it is not what we had in mind, is not complaining. If we complain and become bitter about our situation, those around us will not see Christ. Instead their doubt about our faith in God's timing and answers to prayer will be confirmed and they may reject Christ altogether.

Expectant Thoughts

1. What are some blessings in your life that you can dwell on while waiting for God's answer to your prayer?

2. Why is it important to pray when going through difficult times? God often pairs prayer with casting off anxiety. (Philippians 4:6) Why?

3. Who could you ask to pray with you? Do you seek God daily in prayer for His will concerning your infertility? (Read about Daniel in Daniel 9)

4. Is prayer a priority in your life, or is worry more prevalent? How can you use prayer to replace worry?

Chapter 3: Rachel, A regretful response

"And when the Lord saw that Leah was hated, he opened her womb; but Rachel was barren." Genesis 29:31

I trudged through the mall behind the stroller, debating what I should do. My mother-in-law, sister-in-law and niece were all going shopping in a children's store. Struggling with being unable to conceive children, it was not a place I wanted to be. I decided, against my better judgment, to tough it out and go in. After all, how bad could it be? I walked around trying to look interested, but not too interested in order to avoid the sales people. I was imagining my future daughter in a beautiful purple dress and fighting back tears, when a woman I knew from high school approached me from behind and began the usual onslaught of questions. After the first barrage of "how many kids do you have?", "when are you ever going to have any?" and "why not?", she asked the most horrible question I have ever been asked. "What is wrong with you?"

I am certain Rachel asked herself this question countless times. In no way am I placing blame on Rachel for her infertility. The cause of Rachel's infertility is hard, if not impossible to understand, except to say it was God's plan. Rachel was the favored wife of Jacob. She was the desire of his heart and according to scripture she was beautiful. As the story goes, Jacob was going to work for Laban and was asked what he would want in return. Jacob wanted to marry Rachel. Once this period was over, he expected the father to live up to his agreement. Instead he was fooled into believing that Leah was Rachel and unwittingly he married her instead. Jacob eventually married Rachel as well, and you can imagine the awkwardness of that situation. As we see from the above verse, Leah was able to bear children for Jacob, but Rachel was left barren. Reading through the passage there is no evidence that Rachel did anything that would cause her to be barren. In fact we do not see Rachel even complaining when her beloved Jacob married her sister. The lesson to those of us struggling with barrenness, is in her response when she discovered she could not have children and Leah could.

"And when Rachel saw that she bare Jacob no children, Rachel envied her sister; and said unto Jacob, Give me children or else I die." Genesis 30:1

I do not believe Rachel was making a threat of suicide. I believe she felt like dying because she felt useless and empty. Using Strong's concordance, I broke down this verse and discovered that it is saying that Rachel began to stew about how she was unable to give Jacob any children and she became jealous of her sister. She then demanded that Jacob commit to figuring out a way for her to have a child or she would feel and act as if she no longer existed. In addition to this, the word "die" in this verse means "to execute" or "kill". The feelings of emptiness and uselessness in infertility can be overwhelming. The verse goes on to tell of Jacob's response to this powerful statement. *"And Jacob's anger was kindled against Rachel: and he said, am I in God's stead, who hath withheld from thee the fruit of the womb?"(Genesis 30:2)* What a response. I think my husband and I had a similar conversation: Me: "I just don't understand why this is happening. What is the point in even being a woman if I can't be a mom?" Him: "Why do you keep taking it out on me? It's not my fault we can't have kids." Sound familiar?

In most women the desire to become a mother is so strong that many who find they cannot have children become depressed and full of despair. I believe this is what happened in Rachel's case. She even felt as if her own husband did not care that she was childless and she demands that he give her children. Eventually she resorts to having her handmaid be a sort of surrogate for her. She Leah both seem to be in competition for how many children they can bear for Jacob through their handmaids.

Rachel went looking for her own answers. This is similar to the situation in which Sarah, promised children through Abraham, attempted to fulfill God's promise through her handmaid Hagar. Rachel is similar to many people who, when confronted with infertility, go to every other source but God. Nowhere do we see Rachel seeking God and crying out to Him for His will. Doctors most definitely have their place. I don't believe that medical intervention is unbiblical. But when these avenues are explored before God's will is sought, it can lead to a difficult road. The bible is not clear as to what the spiritual outcome was for Rachel, but He did bless her with a child in His timing and for His greater purpose. *"And God remembered Rachel, and God hearkened to her, and opened her womb,*

And she conceived and bare a son; and said, God hath taken away my reproach: And she called his name Joseph..." Genesis 30:22-24

This is a lesson to us when we see all of our friends and family who have no trouble conceiving. It is tempting to isolate ourselves and become bitter and envious of others. This is especially hard when those who seem to not deserve children have no problems baring them.

"Except the LORD build the house, they labour in vain that build it:" Psalm 127:1

One of the most important lessons to be learned is that no matter what seems like the answer to our problems, God often has other plans. We can try all we want to go outside of the will of God and make things the way we want them, but unless God is the foundation of our family before and after we have children, or even if we never have children, our family will not be successful.

Expectant Thoughts

1. What is one time you have responded wrongly to your circumstances?
2. How can you check your attitude to avoid responding inappropriately? (1 Corinthians 15)
3. What are some ways that we try to control the outcome of our life?
4. What type of family does God think is successful? (Ephesians 6; Colossians 3)

Chapter 4
Pharaoh's Daughter, Compassion to Foster

"And the daughter of Pharaoh came down to wash herself at the river; and her maidens walked along by the river's side; and when she saw the ark among the flags, she sent her maid to fetch it. And when she had opened it, she saw the child: and, behold, the babe wept. And she had compassion on him..." Exodus 2:5-6

Foster care is above all else, about compassion. It is taking a child into your home that may or may not return to their biological family. It is knowing what was done to that child and still working with the family to see them reunited. In this biblical scenario, Moses' mother sent her infant son into the path of Pharaoh's daughter because, at the time, all Hebrew male children were being killed. Pharaoh's daughter took the child and began to raise him as her own.

"In which time Moses was born, and was exceeding fair, and nourished up in his father's house three months: And when he was cast out, Pharaoh's daughter took him up, and nourished him for her own son." (Acts 7:20-21)

It is clear from this passage that Pharaoh's daughter cared for Moses and raised him with love. Like the foster care system, there was also a continued relationship with the birth family. *"Then said his sister to Pharaoh's daughter, Shall I go and call to thee a nurse of the Hebrew women, that she may nurse the child for thee? And Pharaoh's daughter said to her, Go. And the maid went and called the child's mother. And Pharaoh's daughter said unto her, Take this child away, and nurse it for me, and I will give thee thy wages. And the women took the child, and nursed it."* (Exodus 2:7-9)

Children in the foster care system still care about their birth family. Just as Moses was able to connect with his birth family, it is important for foster children to connect with their birth family in some way if possible.

Having said this, foster care is not a position to be entered into lightly. Having compassion for children is one aspect of fostering, but so is being able to have boundaries. In this biblical example, Moses was fostered because there was a danger to his life if he were to remain with his birth family. Such is the case with many children in the foster care system. However, the threat to children in foster care is usually *because* of their birth family. This can be a huge psychological barrier.

I will not go into all of the aspects of foster care and how it works and what kind of children go into care. If you are genuinely interested, I highly recommend attending trainings and meetings at your local agency or Department of Human Services—but beyond just garnering information; I implore you to seek the face of God on this matter. The fact is that if you desire to have children in your home to love and care for and who will love you back and be a part of your family, foster care may not be for you. I said *may* not. The children whom you will encounter may be capable of giving and receiving love right away. But they also may not be. Couples experiencing infertility must be certain that God wants them to be involved with the foster care system. Here are some things you may want to consider:

1. The children you are fostering may not ever be eligible for adoption. This includes infants, who in most states must be in your home for a certain length of time, and parental rights terminated, before they can be adopted. This means that you could care for a child from birth until they are old enough to call you "ma-ma" and "dada" and then have to watch them returned to their birth family.

2. Children in the foster care system are often from very broken families. Older children especially may not trust you and may lash out and hurt you in the deepest of ways.

3. Foster care is just that; foster care. The word 'foster' is defined in the dictionary as "to promote the growth or development of; further; encourage." In most cases it is temporary and reunification is the ultimate goal. Using these children as a replacement for what you cannot have is unwise and unhealthy for everyone. What they need is unconditional love from a family that does not expect anything in return.

4. Through foster care your life will become an open book to social workers and other state employees. The biblical discipline of spanking that many Christian families implement has no place in the foster care system, as many of these children come from backgrounds of unspeakable abuse. God has a purpose in even the darkest of situations.

As Pharaoh's daughter raised Moses, it became clear that his separation from his birth family was for a specific God-ordained purpose. No other Hebrew could have simply marched into Pharaoh's palace and demanded that he let God's people go. Moses had a relationship with Pharaoh and was able to demonstrate God's power because of the situation that God allowed. This goes to show that you never know who you will foster or adopt. Just as Moses was used greatly of God, all children, biological, adopted or fostered, can just as easily be used.

Expectant Thoughts

1. How can you see evidence of God's planning in Moses' life?
2. In what ways would fostering children affect your household?
3. How could things have turned out differently in Moses' life if Pharaoh's daughter had not had compassion on him?
4. What does the Bible say about compassion? (Psalm 86:15; Psalm 111:4; Matthew 9:36; Matthew 18:33; Luke 10:33; 1 Peter 3:8; 1 John 3:17)

Chapter 5
Samson's Mother, God is in Control

"And there was a certain man of Zorahm of the family of the Danites, whose name was Manoah; and his wife was barren, and bare not." Judges 13:2

There is no name given to this woman in the bible, but she and her husband are demonstrated to be godly people who served God and loved Him. God in His foreknowledge knew the kind of man that Samson would be and knew that He must give him good godly parents who would counsel him wisely. He had several plans for Samson and knew that in order for his plan to be accomplished, it must be at the right time.

"And the angel of the Lord appeared unto the woman, and said unto her, BEHOLD NOW, THOU ART BARREN, AND BEAREST NOT: BUT THOU SHALT CONCEIVE, AND BEAR A SON." Judges 13:3

In verse 5 of Judges 13, it states one purpose for Samson's life: *"...and he shall begin to deliver Israel out of the hand of the Philistines."* God's promise to Manoah and his wife is fulfilled in verse 24: *"And the woman bare a son and called his name Samson: and the child grew, and the Lord blessed him."* Judges 13:24

God's purpose for Samson was to be a judge for Israel and to help free the Israelites from the Philistines.

Samson was also the first Nazarene that we see in the Bible. Samson's hair was the source of his strength. God commanded that it not be cut. If you have ever seen a woman who has never cut her hair, it is pretty amazing. It has to be difficult to take care of and it must get in the way a lot. Just like Samson's hair, our infertility is often difficult to handle and it certainly gets in the way of a 'normal' life. But what if this is our gateway to strength in God? God may be using it to give us the ability to rely on Him. Throughout Samson's life from his miracle conception to his sacrificial death, we see that God is always in control. The book of Hebrews mentions many people that are to be revered as heroes and heroines because of their faith and godly lives.

*"And what shall I more say? for the time would fail me to tell of Gedeon, and of Barak, and of **Samson**, and of Jephthae; of David also, and Samuel, and of the prophets: Who through faith subdued kingdoms, wrought righteousness, obtained promises, stopped the mouths of lions." (Hebrews 11:32-33)*

Samson ultimately found himself at the end of his life because he tried to control his own destiny rather than to let God show Him the way. He gave in to worldly desires and the lusts of the flesh. In the end, however, he perished while taking with him a group of ungodly people who would not hearken to the word of God. Though he failed to fully follow God's will for his life while he was alive, he died serving God.

"For I know the thoughts that I think toward you, saith the LORD, thoughts of peace, and not of evil, to give you an expected end." Jeremiah 29:11

God knows how your life will play out. He knows the choices we will make. His desire is to see us make choices that are in His will, to give us peace. We may wonder why God is not giving us peace in our battle with infertility. Look within and search yourself. Are you resisting God's control of your life? Are you trying to make things go the way you want them to? Like Samson, you may be holding on to things that will cut the source of your strength off, so that God cannot give you the peace about your life and His will for it. Let God convict you and reveal it to you.

Expectant Thoughts

1. How can we give control of our life to God? (Psalm 29:11)

2. What is required of us in order to make God our strength?

3. Are you resisting God's control over your life?

4. How can your infertility bring you closer to God and be used as a gateway to His strength and life-changing power?

5. Are you holding on to anything that is preventing you from having a full relationship with Jesus Christ?

Chapter 6
Hannah, A heart for God

"There was a certain man of Ramathaim-zophim, of mount Ephraim, and his name was Elkanah, the son of Jeroham...And he had two wives; the name of the one was Hannah, and the name of the other Peninnah: and Peninnah had children, but Hannah had no children." 1 Samuel 1:1-2

I remember the day I found out I was going to be an aunt as clearly as it was yesterday. I was in my sister's apartment and had gone to get something for my mom from the living room. Everyone else was over at my mom's house. I was passing the entertainment center when I noticed a card displayed on the top that was obviously for a mother. Thinking to myself, *my sister is not a mom --I wonder what this is?* I grabbed the card and began to read although in the instant I picked it up, I knew. At that point in time, my husband and I had been trying to have children for two years. My sister's pregnancy was unplanned. I went to my mom afterwards and asked her point blank if my sister was pregnant. She said yes. The most difficult part of this situation for me is that they did not want to tell me because they were afraid I would be angry. And I was. I was angry because everyone hid it from me. I was angry because she did not even try. I was angry because I was afraid I would never have children. My sister and I had a rocky relationship growing up, but in recent times had really began to grow closer as she and I both became closer to God. When I found out that she was expecting, I did not understand why God would allow this to happen. In the biblical story of Hannah, she certainly does not understand why God has allowed Elkanah's other wife to be a mother but not herself. She feels as though she is being attacked and is constantly plagued by thoughts from Satan that she is not good enough. *"And her adversary also provoked her sore, for to make her fret, because the LORD had shut up her womb."* (1 Samuel 1:6) *"And she was in bitterness of soul, and prayed unto the Lord, and wept sore"* (1 Samuel 1:10)

Hannah not only had to learn to deal with Penninah's pregnancies, but also the children around her that represented what she could not give her husband. Throughout Hannah's struggle, we see her growing closer to God and wanting to serve Him.

Have you ever heard about the five stages of grief? I believe that infertility is a grieving process and is no different than any other loss, or any other thing we might grieve. Hannah goes thorough many emotions in her struggle with infertility. The first stage of grieving we see in this story is that Elkanah (and possibly Hannah) are in denial. He gives her a "worthy portion" even though she has no children. This also shows his love for her. Often our husbands do not really know how to show their grief in infertility. Denial is more common in men struggling with infertility because the 'problem' is not immediate. They do not deal with the monthly hormone changes directly and all of the physical reminders that infertility brings so they can more easily put it aside. It comes out when they try to satisfy themselves by buying 'things' and consoling their wife with the fact that we own those 'things'.

Depression, although not the 'next step' in the grieving process, can be seen as Hannah begins to refuse to eat. *"And as he did so year by year, when she went up to the house of the Lord, so she provoked her; therefore she wept and did not eat." (1 Samuel 1:7)* Here we see that Hannah has simply given up. Women are more prone to linger in this stage of grief than men. It is easier to shut down than it is to keep going and push the matter aside. Serious physical depression should be looked at by a medical professional. This said, there is nothing too big for God. The word 'depression' does not occur in the Word of God. The closest words to express this state are 'distress' and 'sorrow of heart'. In 2 Samuel 22:7 we read *"In my distress I called upon the Lord, and cried to my God..."* Also we can read in Nehemiah 2:2 after the sepulchers of his father had been destroyed and he wanted to rebuild the walls of Jerusalem that Nehemiah was very depressed *"Wherefore the king said unto me Why is thy countenance sad seeing thou art not sick? This is nothing else but sorrow of heart..."* Spiritual depression is a very powerful thing. It is a pit that is very difficult to get out of. It can contribute to physical ailments and make you more prone to a weak immune system. If we allow it to dominate our thoughts and life, it can soon control us completely. Anxiety is also generally a part of depression and can feed it until it becomes very hard to let go of. While physical depression may have neurological and biological implications, I believe that it usually begins with spiritual depression. It is important if you feel yourself slipping into this state, to seek God and ask Him to lift the depression from you.

The next thing we can see is the anger. *"Then said Elkanah her husband to her, Hannah, why weepest thou? and why eatest thou not? and why is thy heart grieved? am not I better to thee than ten sons?" (1 Samuel 1:8)* Once again, he is trying to console her with what she already has. He is angry and does not know how to fix the situation, so he supplies her with an answer that at the very least, makes her feel guilty and invalidated. Many people around us who know that we are struggling with infertility will try to point out the things we do have. While we should be thankful for the many blessings God gives us, these people do not understand that infertility is a grieving process just like the loss of a loved one. If a friend or relative dies, typically no one will try to point out all the things we have left. It is okay to grieve the loss of a child you may never know. Another step in this grieving process is bargaining. We can see Hannah begin to bargain with God; *"And she vowed a vow, and said, O LORD of hosts, if thou wilt indeed look on the affliction of thine handmaid, and remember me, and not forget thine handmaid, but wilt give unto thine handmaid a man child, then I will give him unto the LORD all the days of his life, and there shall no razor come upon his head."*(1 Samuel 1:11) While we bargain with God by promising Him different things, I do not believe this is how Hannah bargained with God. At first, it may have been out of desperation, but I believe that as she prayed, she realized that she had to give the child that she prayed for to God before

He could bless her with a child. In our lives, it is important to give our children (present and future) to God to use however He wants. They are loaned to us to raise in the "nurture and admonition of the Lord." (Ephesians 6:4) Deal making with God is dangerous and is not what God wants. He wants our willingness and obedience. As Hannah is confronted by Eli the priest who accused her of being drunk, she tells him; *"I am a woman of a sorrowful spirit: I have drunk neither wine nor strong drink, but have poured out my soul before the LORD. Count not thine handmaid for a daughter of Belial: for out of the abundance of my complaint and grief have I spoken hitherto."(1 Samuel 1:15-16)* The word 'complaint' in this verse means 'meditation and the word 'grief' means 'frustration' or 'anger'. Hannah is at a dead end. She has poured herself out to God and has nowhere else to go. It is so often that we wait until there is nothing more that we can do before we ask for God's help. It is imperative that we learn to lean on God in all situations. Hannah learned this by all evidence, in one church service. Who knows how many years it took her to come to the point where she could truly go to God and ask Him for what she wanted, giving it all to Him and expecting nothing in return.
"For this child I prayed; and the Lord hath given me my petition which I asked of him" 1 Samuel 1:27

The final stage in the grieving process is acceptance. It is one not easily attained and it is impossible without the grace of God. We will never truly accept what God does have for us until we first give Him what we don't have.

As the day my sister was to deliver grew closer I found myself in denial. I kept thinking that sooner or later I would have to stop telling myself 'she's just getting fat'. It so happened that at the same time, my sister-in-law, a youth pastor's wife and several other friends were also expecting. My world was turned upside down--or so I thought. Finally the day arrived for my nephew to be born. It was an intense labor and delivery that ultimately resulted in a C-section and thankfully a healthy baby and mom. As I followed everyone to the nursery, I began to feel a dread that I had not expected to feel. I did not want to look at the baby. I did not want to hold him or touch him or see him at all. I felt so guilty for these feelings, because I thought something was wrong with me. Later, I realized that I was so terrified that my feelings during my sister's pregnancy would carry over to my nephew that I wanted to avoid him. I *wanted* to like him--I *wanted* to love him and I was afraid that I would not be able to. I waited until everyone else had looked through the glass, and then I forced myself to look. At the moment I saw him, it all just melted away--the jealousy, the pain, the anger. Though my infertility was still there, and the pain was down deep inside me, I saw my little nephew lying there and somehow God just whispered--here is your 'little man'. He needs an aunt that does not have any children right now. And in my heart I knew that it was true. I believe it was at that moment that I became okay with remaining a family of two.

Expectant Thoughts

1. How was Hannah's bitterness keeping her from a relationship with both God and her husband?
2. What did Hannah miss out on when she was dwelling in her own state of bitterness?

3. What thoughts and feelings are you making yourself feel guilty for?
4. Have you given any future children God may bless you with to Him without condition? If you are unable to have children, have you given Him your life?

Chapter 7
Elisabeth, God's Perfect timing

"And they had no child, because that Elisabeth was barren, and they both were now well stricken in years." Luke 1:7

The birth of John the Baptist is a beautiful example of God's perfect timing in even the most difficult circumstances. Elisabeth and her husband had been dealing with infertility for years and had most likely given up on ever having children. They had learned to become content as a family of two. In this chapter of the book of Luke, there is evidence that people around them felt that Elisabeth and Zacharias were somehow responsible for their own infertility. In verse 36, it says that Elisabeth was "called barren", and in verse 25, Elisabeth says that God has "taken away [her] reproach among men." Now up there in years, they were a good godly couple and there is no evidence that suggests that they could not have children for any other reason than that God wanted to use them to parent the man that would be the forerunner of Jesus Christ. In fact the bible specifically says: *"And they were both righteous before God, walking in all the commandments and ordinances of the Lord blameless." (Luke 1:6)* When the angel came to Mary and told her that she was with child of the Holy Ghost, he also told her of her cousin Elisabeth. *"And behold, thy cousin Elisabeth she hath also conceived a son in her old age; and is the sixth month with her, who was called barren. For with God nothing shall be impossible."* Luke 1:36-37

There are several key words in this verse. The first is the word "was". It indicates that Elisabeth was at one time called barren by others. Perhaps other women talked about her and discussed why she was unable to bear children. Maybe they thought that she or her husband had done something wrong to deserve this barrenness. By saying "was" the angel indicates that no longer will she be called barren. The next is the word "shall" It could have said nothing *is* impossible, but *shall* indicates both the present and future. God has not only used two godly people to parent one of the greatest men on earth, but also to show that though infertile and past child bearing years, nothing is or ever will be impossible for Him.

"And thou shalt have joy and gladness; and many shall rejoice at his birth. For he shall be great in the sight of the Lord..." (Luke 1:13-15)

Elisabeth was six months ahead of Mary in her pregnancy. God had timed her conception perfectly with His will that her son John be able to preach Christ's coming and at the same time experience it.

I can't help but to stop and think about God's perfect timing in my life. There are so many things that would never have happened if I had not had to go through some difficult situations. The first example that comes to my mind is my parent's divorce. Growing up my father's job required us to move from time to time. It eventually led us to Michigan. This is where we lived when my parent's separated. My father lived here for a while, but eventually moved again because of his job, and my mother stayed in Michigan with us. We all know that the ideal situation for children is a two parent home (with a father and a mother). However, God in His foreknowledge knew that my parents would divorce and so planned our lives accordingly. It was here in Michigan that I met my future husband and began attending church with his family. It was at that church that I received assurance of my salvation. I can honestly say that if my parent had not divorced I may not be trying to live for God the way I am now.

The road through infertility may be long and difficult to traverse, but God knows where it will end. In fact He has the ending all planned out. It is our job to use the 'Road Map' He gave us to make sure that we find it.

Expectant Thoughts

1. Are you using God's word as a road map daily to find your way through life?
2. Think on some previously difficult circumstances in your life. What are some positive or God-guided outcomes that have resulted from them?
3. Read Jeremiah chapter 1. What does God say about how well He knows us? What are some things in Jeremiah's life that he gave God control of?
4. Read Psalm 25.
   What are some characteristics of people that God guides?

Chapter 8
Michal, Looking for Fault in Others

"And as the ark of the Lord came into the city of David, Michal Saul's daughter looked through a window, and saw king David leaping and dancing before the Lord; and she despised him in her heart." 2 Samuel 6:16

This is a subject that is sensitive for many who are experiencing infertility. There are those who may feel that God has cursed them with being unable to bear children. The truth of this matter is that our God is a merciful God and gives men many chances to redeem themselves from sin, though none of us deserve it. However, He is also a just God and must judge our sin, particularly sin that is deliberate and unabsolved. There are few times in the bible where God has caused people and nations to remain childless as a last resort in severe instances of incest and adultery.

The only time in the bible where God seems to have 'cursed' someone specific with infertility is in the case of David's wife, Michal. The bible says in the verse above that Michal "despised" David in her heart. If you research this word, despise, in the bible you will find it to mean a willful ignorance of God's plan or an inner disdain and absolute rejection of a person or thing. In other words, Michal found David's rejoicing to the Lord as a negative thing and felt it was beneath the king to rejoice with common people. This is an issue of pride in Michal's life. It also calls to question her faith in God. We can almost hear her contempt for her husband as he returns to her household:

"Then David returned to bless his household. And Michal the daughter of Saul came out to meet David and said, How glorious was the king of Israel to day, who uncovered himself to day in the eyes of the handmaids of his servants as one of the vain fellows shamelessly uncovereth himself!" 2 Samuel 6:20

The bible goes on to say that Michal remained unable to have children.

"Therefore Michal the daughter of Saul had no child unto the day of her death." 2 Samuel 6:23

Even in this scenario, it is unclear if the reason for her infertility was a result of her rejection of the things of God, or because she and king David no longer wished to be with each other. In any case it is unwise and unhealthy to assume that infertility is a punishment for a sin. A tender heart, especially one that has endured criticism and thoughtless comments of others, will certainly question whether she has done something to displease God and make herself barren. Judging the inner thoughts and habits of others based on what we can see outwardly is a natural, and sinful tendency for all mankind. It seems that womankind is perhaps even more inclined to this though. I am not going to proclaim, as some people do, that God would never allow infertility as a consequence for a person's lifestyle choices. That would be foolishness. But I will say that it is probably those who suffer with anxiety over what they may have done wrong, that have the least to worry about. As hard as it may be, try to look past the scrutiny of those around you and be truthful to yourself. Ask God to show you where you are too harsh with yourself and also where you may need to improve some things about your relationship with Him. Do not relate it to your infertility but rather use this circumstance to allow God to help you grow. We can only look within ourselves and decide if *our* lifestyle would be pleasing to God and follow Him in everything we do. Michal, at this point in her life could not have cared less about God. She was very self-focused. But even in the case of Michal, God blessed her with five adopted children.

*"...and the five sons of Michal the daughter of Saul, whom she brought up **for** Adriel the son of Barzillai the Meholathite."* 2 Samuel 21:8

One of my favorite verses in the Bible speaks so beautifully of what Jesus Christ offers us. If you struggle with anxiety and question your worth to God, I encourage you to memorize this verse: *"There is therefore now no condemnation to them which are in Christ Jesus our Lord."(Romans 8:1)*

Expectant Thoughts

1. Do you seek to find fault in others because of your circumstances?

2. Do you have any sin that stands in the way of

God working in your life spiritually while you are going through infertility?

3. Whether or not God allowed you to become pregnant would you be willing to adopt or foster children if He led you to do so?

4. What can you do to please God in your life without children right now?

Chapter 9
The Shunammite Woman, Demonstrating God's Goodness

"And it fell on a day, that Elisha passed to Shunem, where was a great woman; and she constrained him to eat bread."
2 Kings 4:8

The first thing I noticed about this unnamed Shunammite woman is that the Bible calls her 'great'. The word 'great' here means, older or distinguished. *"And he said unto him, Say now unto her, Behold thou hast been careful for us with all this care what is to be done for thee? wouldest thou be spoken for to the king, or to the captain of the host? And she answered, I dwell among mine own people. And he said, What then is to be done for her? and Gehazi answered, Verily she hath no child, and her husband is very old."* 2 Kings 4:13-14

This woman has taken it upon herself to care for the men of God in any way that she can. Having no children of her own, she most certainly still has motherly instincts. Though you may not have children in your home, God intends for you to use your motherly nature to care for those around you. The Shunammite woman was 'great' in that she understood this. She most definitely never said to herself

"What has God done for me; Why should I do anything for Him?" Instead she used her nature to care for others around her. In fact, she never asked for Elisha to give her a child. She remained humble and asked for nothing in return for her kindness. I heard it said once that "every child deserves an aunt and uncle who have no children of their own". Many of us may be able to remember someone like this in our lives that seemed to take great care for us. When we learn to appreciate God's goodness in our lives, despite our circumstances, it is then that we truly know how to be good to others.

"And the woman conceived and bare a son at that season that Elisha had said unto her, according to the time of life."
2 Kings 4:17

Expectant Thoughts

1. Do you question God's plan for your life or find yourself feeling betrayed by Him?
2. If given the opportunity do you use your desire to care for a child to care for others?
3. Do you go out of your way to use the time you have to help those around you who God wants you to minister to?
4. Do you ask God humbly for children or with a selfish attitude? (This does not necessarily change God's answer to your prayer, but it does change your outlook on His response.)

Chapter 10
Esther, A Future Designed by God

"Now in Shushan the palace there was a certain Jew, whose name was Mordecai, the son of Jair, the son of Shimei, the son of Kish, a Benjamite…And he brought up Hadassah, that is, Esther, his uncle's daughter: for she had neither father nor mother, and the maid was fair and beautiful; whom Mordecai, when her father and mother were dead, took for his own daughter." Esther 2:5 and 7

This story is the most detailed biblical account of a physical adoption. In this account, Mordecai is not suffering from infertility that we are aware of, but simply decides to adopt his cousin (his uncle's daughter) Esther, after her parents had died. We do not see any account of Mordecai's wife in this story, however, so it is safe to say that he has none. As the story goes, the king decides that all eligible young women are to be brought to the palace so that he may choose one of them to be his new queen. Hadassah, later called Esther to avoid revealing her Jewish origins, is included in this group of women and so leaves her cousin Mordecai who has cared for her to live in the palace. After she is taken away to live in the palace, he keeps up with her.

"Mordecai walked every day before the court of the women's house, to know how Esther did, and what should become of her." Esther 2:11

If you continue reading this remarkable story, it is one that can be treasured by millions of children who are welcomed into families through adoption. Some children who are adopted struggle with feelings of insecurity, especially if adopted at an older age. Some struggle with acceptance and issues of feeling as if they do not belong. God placed Esther right where she needed to be. Though she went through the heartache of losing her parents, she found another family in her cousin Mordecai. There are many children waiting for families around the world, just like Esther. Adoption is something that is not just a 'good thing to do', it is something that God speaks very highly of. Many times in His word He speaks of caring for the fatherless.

After Esther was taken to the palace, she obtained the favor of her caretaker first and then many others. Ultimately she obtained the favor of the king and fulfilled God's design for her life to deliver His people when she became queen. Perhaps the most well-known verse from this story can be found in Esther 4:14: *"... who knoweth whether thou art come to the kingdom for such a time as this?"* You never know what God's plan is for any child He brings into your life, whether by birth, adoption, fostering, or even teaching Sunday school. God builds families in different ways, but He builds them with the master design blueprint in His hand.

Expectant Thoughts

1. What does God think about adoption according to this story?
2. Read the following verses. How does God feel about those who are orphaned? (Exodus 22:22; Deuteronomy 24:17. 26:12; Psalm 82:3, 146:9; Zechariah 7:10; James 1:27)
3. How can Christians adopting children train more servants for Christ?
4. If Esther's cousin had not raised her in a godly lifestyle, how would this have changed the outcome for the Israelites and for Esther herself?

Chapter 11
Jesus, In All Ways Tempted As We Are

"For we have not an high priest which cannot be touched with the feeling of our infirmities; but was in all points tempted like as we are, yet without sin." (Hebrews 4:15)

Let me start by saying I am not claiming that Jesus wanted physical children. When people say that Jesus knows how we feel and that He experienced the same things we have, it is tempting to say about infertility; "well this is one thing that Jesus did not experience." Jesus Christ was 100% man and 100% God. He not only knows what we have gone through, are going through, and will be going through, he has also experienced the same feelings that we have. Jesus knew His destiny. According to John 18:37, Jesus knew that He was born to die for the sins of mankind. *"Pilate therefore said unto him, Art thou a king then? Jesus answered, Thou sayest that I am a king. To this end was I born, and for this cause came I into the world, that I should bear witness unto the truth."*

Most people, if they are honest with themselves, will say that they do not want to die lonely. God created man so that He would not have to be alone. God created woman so that man would not have to be alone. The need for companionship is innate in man, and I believe it was no different with Jesus. Our desire for children is a God-given desire. Jesus cared for His earthly family and yet He forsook them for His ministry. Most of all, he experienced the rejection of many of the people whom He created. They would never be His children. He knew that they would one day be separated from Him forever. These were things in His life that He experienced that He knew He had to submit to the Heavenly Father about. We see as He prayed in the Garden of Gethsemane that in His humanity He was resistant to the suffering to come: *He went away again the second time, and prayed, saying, O my Father, if this cup may not pass away from me, except I drink it, thy will be done. (Matthew 26:42)*

God sent Jesus to earth to become a man, to live a sinless and pure life. If we believe that the bible is true when it says that he was in all points tempted, yet without sin, we must believe that He experienced things that brought about the same feelings as infertility. As He is also all-knowing, He watches each of us lovingly and grieves for you as He watches you go through your trials. Jesus looked on the multitudes and had compassion. He looked at the Samaritan woman and had compassion. He healed many people from their infirmities because He had the ability and because it served to magnify and glorify God to others. God cares about a small sparrow that falls. How much more does he care for you?

Expectant Thoughts

1. Your circumstance is hard, but your heart does not have to be. How can you look at the life of Christ and strive to become moldable in His hands?
2. For each and every opportunity to choose a poor mental attitude, God provides an opportunity to escape. What plans have you made for yourself in the past? In what ways were those plans different than God's?
3. Jesus wants to bear your burdens, but he won't take them from you unless you give them to Him willingly. What unnecessary burdens are you bearing?
4. What extra baggage are you carrying around that is weighing down your life and your ability to have a better relationship with your Saviour?

Ten Spiritual Counsels From People Who Have Been There

Chapter 12
Pray Without Ceasing: God as a Resting Place

"Be Careful for nothing; but in everything by prayer and supplication with thanksgiving let your requests be made known unto God." (Philippians 4:6)

One of the best pieces of advice that I was given, that I found the most difficult to practice at times was to pray. Prayer is the way we talk to God. It is God's desire to have us communicate our desires and our praise to Him. In times of unbelievable pain and anguish it can be our only solace and our *"refuge, until these calamities be overpast."* (Psalm 57:1)

Towards the beginning of my struggle with infertility, I realized that what I was actually having the most difficult time with was something that had plagued me for years before my infertility. It was the sin of worrying. Through counsel with our pastor, and a true desire to know God's purpose for our struggle, I began to truly read my bible and pray for God's will and for understanding. I came across the above passage in Philippians and God kept drawing my attention back to it. I could not figure out what it meant. That very week a couple who travel the country preaching and singing in churches, came to our church. They had a book table and on that table was a book titled, "The Sin of Worrying". I knew I struggled with worry and so I bought the book and began to read. Inside to my surprise was the very passage God had been drawing to my attention. *"Be careful for nothing"* means do not worry. It is saying that we should not worry about the outcome of our situation but pray to God and thank Him for His wisdom in knowing what is best for us. In other words: Stop Worrying and Start Praying. Just realizing that God is in control and in His infinite wisdom, He knows what is best for us, took a great weight off of me.

"...In everything by prayer and supplication with thanksgiving..." is the next part of this verse. The storms and trials of life are when we go to Him the most. But we need to go to Him with a thankful heart. This is one of the hardest things to do for most people. The bible says *"In every thing give thanks: for this is the will of God in Christ Jesus concerning you." (1 Thessalonians 5:18)* This means when things are going terrifically, praise and thank Him. It also means that when things are not going so well, we should thank Him too. This is because not only does God want and deserve our thanks and praise, but because He knows what is ultimately the best for us, and we need to acknowledge that by thanking Him in advance. Ecclesiastes 3:1 says *"To every thing there is a season, and a time to every purpose under the heaven."* God has a perfect plan and purpose for everything. He knows everything that is going to happen before it happens. One subject that it is necessary to touch on is that of miscarriage. Since I have never knowingly experienced this, I do not feel qualified to give specific

advice. I can only imagine the heartache and pain that the premature death of a baby can cause. Psalm 107:28-30 says: *"Then they cry unto the LORD in their trouble, and he bringeth them out of their distresses. He maketh the storm a calm, so that the waves thereof are still. Then are they glad because they be quiet; so he bringeth them unto their desired haven."* I believe that bible is addressing those situations and storms in life where we just want to get out of the storm and rest in His peace. Though the pain and memory will surly linger, God can take you and set you in His haven of peace and rest and show you His purpose for your storm. King David's son, Soloman knew about God being a resting place. In the book of 1 Kings, he talks to the children of Israel about rebuilding the temple and it being the dwelling place of God. He also knew that this required much prayer. Verse 54 -56 of chapter 8 says, *"And it was so, that when Solomon had made an end of praying all this prayer and supplication unto the LORD, he arose from before the altar of the LORD, from kneeling on his knees with his hands spread up to heaven. And he stood, and blessed all the congregation of Israel with a loud voice, saying, Blessed be the LORD, that hath given <u>rest</u> unto his people Israel, according to all that he promised: there hath not failed one word of all his good promise, which he promised by the hand of Moses his servant."*

Chapter 13
Read God's Word and Apply it: God as a Buckler

"That your faith should not stand in the wisdom of man, but in the power of God." (1 Corinthians 2:5)

God's word has the power to change our perspective. It is powerful, purposeful, progressive, prospective, panoramic, prophetic, and prudent. It is not, however, always popular. In today's society there seems to be little or no solace for the Christian struggling with infertility. The bible says in Psalm142:4, *"I looked on my right hand, and beheld, but there was no man that would know me: refuge failed me; no man cared for my soul..."* Even inside the church, unless you are surrounded by people who have been there, you become accustomed to comments like "Just relax...", "Just adopt...", "Just go to the doctor...", "Just wait..." In other words, just leave the rest of us alone because we really don't understand. Notice that God does not advise us to wait for man's solution to our problem, or barge ahead and decide what is best for us without His perfect will involved. He tells us to rely on His power, not in what man may think is the right thing to do. This is not to say that medical intervention, adoption or other alternatives to a natural conception are wrong; quite the contrary. While there are some medical methods that I personally find to be against my moral conscience and some that I feel go against bible principles, there are many, many alternate paths for those who are unable to conceive. One important thing to mention is that these alternatives are not *because* you could not become pregnant. Think of infertility as the 'detour' sign in road construction. God's plan for some people is to go a different route when adding to their family. Some examples are foster care, adoption, embryo adoption, and some forms of surgical and pharmaceutical intervention. The idea here is not to say that waiting and waiting for a natural conception to take place when the likelihood is improbable is what we should all do. What we should do is to seek out God's wisdom and try as best as we can to let Him have control of our specific situation.

"Sing, O barren, thou that didst not bear; break forth into singing, and cry aloud, thou that didst not travail with child: for more are the children of the desolate than the children of the married wife, saith the LORD." (Isaiah 54:1)

For some people God's will may be that they remain a family of two. If this is the case, it is important to lean on the Word of God and hold fast to its truths. God has a way of giving us what we want without our knowledge. He knows what is truly best for us, though we may not think so. In the middle of my struggle I found out that it *was* possible to be happy without children in my home. There were children all around me who needed me. My Sunday school class, my nephew, my preschool students, and children in our church...the list goes on and on. In fact because I was not a parent, I was able to spend more time and more energy helping these children than if I was a mother. Don't get me wrong, at the time I would have rather spent my energy on children of my own; but looking back I can see that God wanted me to use my resources and the abilities that He has given me specifically for these children at that time. The verse above rang true for me and if I had never been blessed with children in my home, I know that those multitudes of children were mine to care for as best as I could. In fact, I believe that the love I already had for children was expanded even further by my infertility journey.

    We see countless times in the bible where God's word comes to someone in the midst of their struggles and reassures them with its promises and comfort. Though we may not hear the audible voice of God now, we can certainly still receive His word. Remember Hannah's miracle son, Samuel? In 2 Samuel 22:31 he speaks of the word of God as a buckler: *"As for God, his way is perfect; the word of the LORD is tried: he is a buckler to all them that trust in him"*

Chapter 14
Choose the Right Attitude: God as a Whirlwind

"Great is our Lord and of great power; His understanding is infinite." (Psalm 147:5)

Above all we need to make sure we don't develop a deserving attitude. If we walk around thinking we deserve to have children and others do not, we are being covetous. It is difficult to understand why some people who are neglectful or abusive to their children are able to have them while others who are "good" Christians are not. If I knew the answer, I would not still have a hard time with this. I do believe though, that God needs Christians to be available to provide homes for children who need them. The bible speaks often of caring for the "orphans" and the "fatherless". There are many children who desperately need loving, Christ-centered homes as well as many birthmothers who need to know that they have an alternative to abortion. As for why these children suffer in the first place; the answer is sin. Since the fall of Adam and Eve in the Garden of Eden, sin has been in this world: *"For as by one man sin entered into this world, and death by sin..." (Romans 5:12)*. Many people question God when it comes to trials and tribulations in this life. They often ask how a loving God could allow such things to happen. Jesus himself answers this question in Matthew 18:7 when He says *"Woe unto the world because of offenses! for it must needs be that offenses come; but woe to that man by whom the offense cometh!"* In this world there will be those who transgress against others and God because of sin, but they will be judged. God does not take the abuse of children lightly. This chapter begins by expressly stating how much Jesus hates the sin of child abuse: *"But whoso shall offend one of these little ones which believe in me, it were better for him that a millstone were hanged about his neck, and that he were drowned in the depth of the sea." (Matthew 18:6)* Nevertheless, it is not *our* duty to judge people who seem to have children undeservingly. While child abuse and neglect must not go unreported, or unpunished within the confines of the criminal justice system, becoming hateful over other situations that seem so wrong to us is also wrong and does not please God. It is hard to understand. It is hard to cope with. We do not know God's greater plan for these circumstances. We do know that *"all things work together for good to them that love God..." (Romans 8:28)*

It is hard in the whirlwind of infertility treatments and worries to just focus on one thing at a time. But it is through these whirlwind experiences that God often speaks to us the loudest. Job experienced God's whirlwind, both figuratively as well as literally. God allowed a lot of unfortunate circumstances to come into his life in order to teach him an important lesson on pride. In the end of the book of Job, chapter 38 verse 2, Job hears God speak to him out of a whirlwind saying, *"Who is this that darkeneth counsel by words without knowledge?"* This indicates that there was no understanding behind the counsel that was being given. God spoke loud and clear to Job that day. Nahum 1:3 says *"the LORD hath his way in the whirlwind and in the storm..."* and in verse 7; *"The LORD is good, a strong hold in the day of trouble; and he knoweth them that trust in him."* When it seems that your life is in a whirlwind and there are so many 'undeserving' others out there receiving what you desire, remember the pride of Job who was *"perfect and upright"*(Job 1:1) in the eyes of God, yet went through many hardships and learned a valuable lesson.

Chapter 15
Manifest God Through Your Struggle: God as an Ointment

"Jesus answered, NEITHER HATH THIS MAN SINNED, NOR HIS PARENTS: BUT THAT THE WORKS OF GOD SHOULD BE MADE MANIFEST IN HIM. (John 9:3)

The passage above is from the familiar story of Jesus healing the man born blind. In the story of the man born blind, Jesus is questioned by the disciples as to what sin the man or his parents had committed that he should be born blind. Interestingly enough it is not the Pharisees or Levites that ask this question as in much of the gospels, but Jesus' friends. We see this parallel in our lives as well-meaning (and sometimes not) friends and family ask us to ponder what we have done that God would strike us barren. Jesus' answer in the third verse of John 9 should comfort us greatly. It was not that the man or his parents had sinned, but that God wanted to show Himself to those Jesus was ministering to by healing the man. And, needless to say, if there was no need for healing, there would be no miracle. Unfortunately we often glory in this miracle and focus so much on the healing that we fail to recognize what Jesus really intended as the outcome of this miracle.

I have never experienced a family member with a serious impairment such as blindness, but I have known some close friends who have experienced a similar situation with a child. Going through the journey of infertility I have realized that it is not unlike this type of infirmity. The family struggles with why God would allow such a thing to happen and how much to rely on doctors and how much on God's healing. Infertility is similar in that we struggle with why God has allowed us to go through this and how much we should take our medical options into our own hands, or to just trust God. We must understand though, God may not necessarily want to heal our infertility, though that may happen. It may be just that He wants to use us for His glory and purpose, but cannot do so without allowing us to be barren.

Jesus goes on in this chapter to talk about doing the work of His Father, and healing the man. The medium in which he heals him is quite interesting. He uses clay and spit to rub on the man's eyes so that he is healed. If we were to imagine healing someone by rubbing something on them it probably would not be spit and dirt. However, in our lives it is often the hurtful comments (the spit, if you will) and the pain within (the dirt) that causes us to eventually do the most healing--if we allow it. It is up to us to take the battles we face in our journey of infertility and use them to better ourselves spiritually and glorify God in our daily lives. After Jesus rubbed on the dirt and spit, he told the man to wash in the pool of Siloam. The blind man could have said "No Thanks Jesus. You already rubbed spit and dirt on me. I'm just going to figure out a way to heal myself." Instead, the man born blind went and washed in the pool after the spit and clay were rubbed on his eyes, and he was given his sight. We need to wash in God's word and in prayer and worship of him and we will see eventually what God wants to manifest in our lives.

We see another example of God revealing His power through His Son Jesus in the raising of Lazarus from the dead. The second part of letting God manifest Himself in your infirmity is to allow for His timing. This is perhaps the most difficult part to any struggle that involves a desire for something. We want so badly to have things in our time that we fail to think about what God has in store for us in His time. In the story of Lazarus, it states *"1 Now a certain man was sick, named Lazarus, of Bethany, the town of Mary and her sister Martha...3 Therefore his sisters sent unto him, saying Lord, behold, he whom thou lovest is sick. 4 When Jesus heard that, he said THIS SICKNESS IS NOT UNTO DEATH, BUT FOR THE GLORY OF GOD, THAT THE SON OF GOD MIGHT BE GLORIFIED THEREBY. 5 Now Jesus loved Martha and her sister and Lazarus. 6 When he had heard therefore that he was sick, he abode two days still in the same place where he was."* **(John 11:1, 3-6)**

Most of us upon discovering that we had a sick friend who was close to death, would have immediately rushed to see them. Not Jesus. He knew that Lazarus was sick and dying for a reason. And it was not so he could rush to his side and heal him as he had so many others. He loved Lazarus very much though and it was certainly difficult for him to wait. But he stayed where he was for two more days.

If we look further into the chapter it dispels the

theory that Lazarus was just in a coma or sleeping. Not only had he been in the grave for four days when Jesus arrived, but Jesus says very plainly *"Lazarus is dead."* (John 11:14) He is immediately besieged by Martha who says *"if thou hadst been here, my brother had not died."* (John 11:21) as if Jesus did not know this. He could have healed Lazarus from right where he was and not even come to Bethany to see him. The point of all this is that Jesus knew that this was to demonstrate God's glory and timing in everything. There was to be no question about Lazarus' resurrection. In our day to day struggle with infertility it seems as if *we* need a daily resurrection. Some days we just want God to heal us RIGHT NOW, or to just give us a sign that He never will. In the lives of Mary and Martha they had an immediate problem. Lazarus was dying. They wanted an immediate solution. They wanted Jesus to heal him. God, however, had something greater in store for them. Yes, they had to experience the pain of Lazarus' death. So did Jesus. But it was all to show the greater purpose of God and to give glory to His Son Jesus. Jesus knows how much we hurt. He wants to heal us. God the Father knows when it is time for that to happen. It may not be physically, but emotionally or spiritually. He will wait until the time when His Son can be glorified by the healing. Are you dead spiritually? Let God heal you. Trust in His perfect will and timing for your life.

Chapter 16
Accept Other Alternatives:
God as a Redeemer

"And he said, TAKE NOW THY SON, THINE ONLY SON ISAAC, WHOM THOU LOVEST, AND GET THEE INTO THE LAND OF MORIAH AND OFFER HIM THERE FOR A BURNT OFFERING UPON ONE OF THE MOUNTAINS WHICH I WILL TELL THEE OF." (Genesis 22:2)

There were many times in my struggle with infertility that I told God (as it says in 1 Peter 5:7 and again in Psalm 55:22) that I was giving Him my burden of infertility. I kneeled many times at the altar in our church and cried out within myself, "God I can't bear this burden. I'm giving it to you to carry for me. Tell me what you want me to do." This is, I believe, the first step. I came to realize though that I was giving God my *infertility* and the pain that I could not bear alone, but I had never surrendered to Him my *fertility*. It may seem like an absurd thought at first, but God truly wants *all* of us. So how can a person who is infertile, give God their fertility? The way I looked at it was based on the story of Abraham and Isaac. God told Abraham that he would someday have children, when it seemed impossible, and then He told him to kill his only son as a sacrifice.

Abraham had surrendered his burden of not having children to God and trusted in His ability to see him through the pain. Now, God was asking Him to give Him the one thing he had prayed and asked for originally; his son Isaac. If we give God our pain and burdens, He is able to bear them for us. But God wants to know that we are completely surrendered. I needed to tell God that not only did I trust Him to get me through the hard times and help me cope with the pain of infertility; but that I also was willing to sacrifice having children at all if that was His will. It also entailed sacrificing my will for any future children He might bless us with and saying, "God, if you choose to bless us with children, I understand that they are YOURS, and I will trust you to give me the wisdom to raise them for your honor and purpose." This was a pivotal point in my spiritual life and one I believe I may never have reached without the journey of infertility.

God tells us often in His word that we need to "die to self" in order to live for Him. The apostle Paul himself said *"I die daily" (1 Corinthians 15:31)*. This goes hand in hand with surrendering your burdens <u>and</u> will to God. Like Abraham sacrificed Isaac, God wants us to present our body a living sacrifice to Him: *"I beseech you therefore, brethren, by the mercies of God, that ye present your bodies a living sacrifice, holy, acceptable unto God, which is your reasonable service."* (Romans 12:1)

In John chapter 12:24 the bible says: *"VERILY, VERILY I SAY UNTO YOU, EXCEPT A CORN OF WHEAT FALL INTO THE GROUND AND DIE, IT ABIDITH ALONE: BUT IF IT DIE, IT BRINGITH FORTH MUCH FRUIT."* Jesus is speaking here and telling the people that unless they die to their will and surrender to God's, they will be alone and produce no 'fruit' or works for God. But if they allow God to have complete control, and surrender to His will, they will have 'much fruit' or see many works of God in their lives. In our battle with infertility, it is hard to see that anything good can come of it. But if we let God work how He wants to and give Him 'permission' to have control over our will, then we will see Him work.

Chapter 17
Don't Give in or Give up: God as a Rock

"Jesus said unto him, IF THOU CANST BELIEVE, ALL THINGS ARE POSSIBLE TO HIM THAT BELIEVETH. And straitway the father of the child cried out and said with tears, Lord, I believe, help thou mine unbelief." (Mark 9:23-24)

Few people went through as many hardships in the bible as Joseph. He was born into a family of brothers who hated him because he was the treasured son of Rachel and Jacob. His father gave him a special coat and his brothers plotted to kill him. He was instead sold into slavery and when he thought he had found a good place in the home of Potiphar, he was lied about and thrown into prison. The story can be read in Genesis, but to make a long (and very good) story short; Joseph eventually became a very important person in Pharaoh's house because God gave him the ability to interpret dreams. This God-given ability put him in the position to provide his birth family with food in a time of famine. His forgiving heart towards his brothers is evident as he states in Genesis 50:20 *"But as for you, ye thought evil against me; but God meant it unto good, to bring to pass, as it is this day, to save much people alive."*

We often wonder why so many Christian women who love the Lord seem to go through infertility while others who are lost or do not care about their children have so many. Many argue that God would not want these women to go childless. I argue that perhaps He does—at least for a time. He needs to prepare their hearts, as he did Joseph's, for the time when He would need them to step out in faith and do something to fulfill His will in their lives such as adopting. The last part of the above verse, "to save much people alive", shows that God often designs the lives of certain individuals around a need to preserve the lives of many others. Adoption is a preservation of life. Without its availability how many more abortions and tragic childhood deaths would there be? Certainly God desires for those children to end up in godly homes, and as can be seen in the life of the apostle Paul, God takes a special interest in transforming the most difficult of circumstances into miraculous works to glorify His name.

Another person in the bible who had perhaps even more struggles was Job. Job lost his family, his possessions, his health; everything dear to him, because God knew that he would praise him through the trial. Job said *"But he knoweth the way that I take: when he hath tried me, I shall come forth as gold. "* *(Job 23:10)* Gold must be purified by being heated by fire. It cannot be valuable and pure without the fire. As an imperfect people, we must believe that God is using the hardships in our lives to purify us for His use. God knows that we are weak. Just as the man who wanted his daughter healed asked God to "help [his] unbelief" (Mark 9:24) we need to also ask God to strengthen our belief that he can bring us through our trial. In the book of Isaiah it says: *"Hast thou not known? hast thou not heard, that the everlasting God, the LORD, the Creator of the ends of the earth, fainteth not, neither is weary? there is no searching of his understanding. He giveth power to the faint; and to them that have no might he increaseth strength. Even the youths shall faint and be weary, and the young men shall utterly fall: But they that wait upon the LORD shall renew their strength; they shall mount up with wings as eagles; they shall run, and not be weary; and they shall walk, and not faint." (Isaiah 40:28-31)*

Hannah is perhaps the most descriptive account of someone struggling with infertility in the bible. Her confidence in God was shaken, her husband had little or no comprehension of what she was going through and her priest thought she was a drunk. This feeling of utter abandonment is one that I knew all too well going through infertility. There were so many times when it seemed that everything was hopeless and no one cared. But as Hannah's persistence paid off and she remained true to God, she found out that holding on to the only thing solid and real in her life was what kept her from falling apart completely. *"There is none holy as the Lord: for there is none beside thee: neither is there any rock like our God."* These words prayed by Hannah in 1 Samuel 2:2, clearly show that God's love for us is solid like a rock and if we cling to Him in hard times, he will be an unmovable and steadfast stronghold.

Even Jesus went through many hardships during His years here on earth. God the Father allowed it so that His Son would be 'made perfect' before all when He went to His death on the cross. In Hebrews chapter 5 verses 8 and 9, the bible says *"Though he were a Son, yet learned he obedience by the things which he suffered; And being made perfect, he became the author of eternal salvation unto all them that obey him."* The trials Jesus went through were to prove that He was the Son of God. But the evidence is not in the trials; only in His reaction to them. How we react to trials is evidence to others of where our obedience lies and in whom we put our faith and trust.

The seemingly unreachable mountain of parenthood that so many of us seek can tempt us to look back on our failures and decide to quit. Being stuck in the valley of infertility can get so overwhelming at times that it may seem easier to give up on God than to go forward for Him. Caleb wandered for years with the Israelites in the wilderness. He struggled through poor leadership, idolatry and many other hardships. He knew about giving up. A lot of people around him did just that. But as we can see in Joshua chapter 14:11-12, Caleb kept his eyes on the mountain of God's promise. *"As yet I am as strong this day as I was in the day that Moses sent me: as my strength was then, even so is my strength now, for war, both to go out, and to come in. Now therefore give me this mountain, whereof the LORD spake in that day; for thou heardest in that day how the Anakims were there, and that the cities were great and fenced: if so be the LORD will be with me, then I shall be able to drive them out, as the LORD said."*

Chapter 18

Reach Out to Others: God as a Vine

"And we know that all things work together for good to them that love God..." (Romans 8:28)

One of the most frustrating things about infertility for me, from a social perspective, is that so many people do not understand what it is like to experience such an emotional upheaval in your life. When you go through your day to day interactions with people and the subject of children or pregnancy comes up, you are faced with two basic options: One, you can let people know that you are going through infertility right now; or Two, you can just go along with their conversation and pretend like nothing bothers you. Infertility can become a very *me* centered battle. It is easy to isolate yourself to the point where you avoid all contact with people who have children. While it is understandable to avoid some situations that you know will not be healthy for you such as baby showers or dedications, it is important to realize that driving away everyone and everything that reminds you of your situation is both unhealthy and unrealistic. Choosing to go into denial about your condition is also unhealthy. It is true that it is no one's business but yours and your spouse when it comes to your fertility; but there are ways to bring about awareness to others without embarrassing yourself, your spouse or another brother or sister in Christ. In Luke 13:11 the Bible tells us about a young woman who had a debilitating condition that caused her to be bent over and unable to stand upright all the way: *"And, behold, there was a woman which had a spirit of infirmity eighteen years, and was bowed together, and could in no wise lift up herself."*

    This woman wanted to be healed. She did not ask for this condition, nor was she able to help herself. She no doubt struggled on a daily basis to make sense of her state and desired to be cured and live a normal life. This echoes what many who are facing the trials of infertility go through. They too are 'bowed together' to the point where all they can see is their condition and it is difficult to see anything else. Things seem very discouraging. They want to be healed, to know what it is like to live a 'normal' life and be just like everyone else. The world comes at them with cliché' suggestions and 'easy' answers that only serve to make the person giving the suggestion feel like they are somehow full of wisdom or give them a way to escape a situation they know nothing about. Usually these suggestions begin with "Just..." and continue with some nonsensical piece of advice that does nothing but make the person receiving it feel invalidated and hurt. Many people think that it is never the will of God for someone to be sick or physically impaired. They usually think that because they have never been through anything and so they want to think that they must be doing something right. This is absolutely not true. The book of Job says that *"man is born unto trouble, as the sparks fly upward."* (Job 5:7) The woman in the book of Luke went to the right place to be healed. She turned to Jesus. She also turned to the church, not away from it. Jesus found her in the church: *"And he was teaching in one of the synagogues on the Sabbath...And, behold, there was a woman which had a spirit of infirmity eighteen years, and was bowed together, and could in no wise lift up herself."* (Luke 13:11) She did not allow her infirmity to control her. She kept her eyes focused on God and her desire to serve Him. If we continue to serve God through our suffering, we can be the example that God wants us to be as Christians. Not only will other Christians see our stand for God even through trials, but so will the lost world.

The brokenness produced by the suffering that God allows in the lives of His children is often the most beautiful story of all. I heard a story about a stained glass window of great beauty. It was full of many different colors and pictures. But all it was is broken glass that someone put together to make a piece of art. And when the sun shone through it, it was even more beautiful. Our brokenness can be taken by God and formed into beautiful art. And if we let the Son shine through our brokenness we can let others know about His wonderful love and friendship.

The trials that you go through may be the key that unlocks the door to a new level in your relationship with God. In the book of John, Jesus says, *"I am the true vine, and my Father is the husbandman. Every branch in me that beareth not fruit he taketh away: and every branch that beareth fruit, he purgeth it, that it may bring forth more fruit." (John 15:1-2)* He is comparing himself to a vine, God the Father to the caretaker and us to the branches that grow along the vine. As we go through life, we are a testimony to others through every aspect of our Christian life. We should also be a verbal testimony of Christ and His salvation. As branches, we require pruning to make us grow properly and yield more fruit. Pruning is not always pleasant. It is often painful. It's how we respond to God in these times that truly determine what we will yield for him at harvest time. One more thing that pruning does is bring us closer to the Vine. As we go through trials and lessons that God wants to teach us, we turn to God (or we should) for our source of strength. It is at these times that we are the closest to Christ.

Chapter 19
Wait for Now; Not Tomorrow: God as a Craftsman

"For now we see through a glass darkly, but then face to face, now I know in part, but then shall I know even as I am also known." (I Corinthians 5:17)

Infertility hurts. There's no way around that. In the middle of it all, the patronizing platitudes of others sting like the proverbial 'salt' in our wounded hearts. However, if you look closely at scripture, salt actually has a higher place on the shelf of our lives. The bible says in Matthew 5:13, *"Ye are the salt of the earth..."*

Salt in those days, and still in ours, was used not only as a flavoring, but as a preservative. While I realize that the salt in this verse is referring to us and our usefulness to God, if we look at it in the context of this example, we could say that the journey of infertility is wrought with opportunities to use the salt that others throw at us as faith 'preservers' instead of faith 'flavorers'. If we spend our time waiting for tomorrow and worrying about the next trial, we may miss God's plan for us today. God knows what lies in wait for us. Often we try to flavor our faith by taking the salt and rubbing it deeper in to 'make us stronger' for the future. While it is true that these experiences can make us stronger, it is only if we learn to lean on God that we receive the right kind of strength. Use God as your preserver and lean wholly on Him today to strengthen your faith in a permanent way. Then you will see what God wants to use you for in the future. Through a study of infertility in the bible we have seen that God used infertility to teach His people many important lessons. He also used it, in part, to lead to the generation that produced His Son Jesus Christ who ultimately died for the sins of mankind. So the next time someone hurls those tiring, hurtful phrases at you, respond, with love, "I don't know how God wants to use my situation, but I know He has a perfect plan for me." And believe it for yourself. A good friend once told me that the journey of infertility is like an embroidery project being worked on by God. While we are going through it, we see it from behind--a knotted tangled mess. But if we let God keep on working, when He is finished we will see how beautiful His design is.

Chapter 20
Don't Let in Bitterness: God as a Mountain

"And she was in bitterness of soul, and prayed unto the Lord, and wept sore." (I Samuel 1:10)

One of the most powerful and all encompassing sins is bitterness. I am so very thankful that a godly friend warned me of this at the very beginning of my struggle with infertility. Bitterness is something that I believe everyone struggles with on some level. The important thing is not to let it take root in your life. It is one of those sins that has a way of sneaking in. Some infraction occurs towards us and we dwell on it and think on it, and do not ask for God's wisdom or go to the person who hurt us and talk to them, instead we bury it inside and plant the seed of bitterness within our heart. From this point on, the seed of bitterness will begin to take root and soon anything that the person says or does will be wrong or bothersome. Then, any thing or situation that reminds us of our problem will start to bother us, and we will react in irrational and angry ways. Some of the fruits, or results of bitterness can be: anger, hatred, sarcasm, gossip, slander, covetousness, jealousy, rebellion, depression and eventually spiritual death. There are many, many more fruits of bitterness, but these are just a few. In the passage above Hannah is struggling with infertility and is weeping and praying before God. Her **soul** is bitter. If you think of the seed of bitterness producing a root and then a vine that creeps around inside us, it may help. I believe that the vine of bitterness starts with our flesh, or body. It begins by a human remark or circumstance. We take it in and let it stand. Hannah had already taken her situation of infertility and her husband's other wife's ability to conceive and given the root of bitterness a place in her heart. The next place it travels is our soul. The soul is the crossroads of communication between us and God. This passage in 1 Samuel goes on in verse 11 to describe Hannah's desire for a child. She vows to God that she will do whatever needs to be done to make it happen. In James 4:3 it states: *"Ye ask, and receive not, because ye ask amiss, that ye may consume it upon your lusts."* Though her intentions seem to be very well-meaning, it is questionable whether or not Hannah has let her desires overwhelm her need to be in the will of God. But I believe it is often necessary to voice our mind, our will and our desires to God in order to empty us of *self.* In verse 15, Hannah states *"...I have poured out my soul before the Lord..."* The soul is where we receive redemption and the forgiveness of our sins. It is at this point that I believe Hannah realized where she was headed. She came before God and confessed her bitterness and asked for His help. In James 4:9-10 it says: *"Be afflicted, and mourn, and weep: let your laughter be turned to mourning, and your joy to heaviness. Humble yourselves in the sight of the Lord, and he shall lift you up."*

If we allow the vine of bitterness to grow, it will eventually enter into our spirit and to spiritual death. If we are saved, we have God's Spirit to bear witness with our own spirit.(Romans 8:16)   Hannah's spirit at this point in time was "sorrowful". We cannot have bitterness in our soul and have a contented spirit. After her surrender to God and her discussion with Eli, the priest, Hannah went away and her countenance, or appearance, was no longer "sad". Hannah could have made a lot of different choices. She could have simply complained to God and let the bitterness continue to spread from her soul into her spirit. She could have then said "Well, God isn't helping me, so I'm going to try idol worship." This bitter and rebellious attitude would have perhaps even led to spiritual death.

    Bitter roots produce bitter fruits. I mentioned above some of the fruits of bitterness. In contrast to the story of Hannah, a godly woman who realized she was harboring the root of bitterness, and confessed it before it was too late; the story of Jacob and Esau shows what can happen if we allow bitterness to take over our lives. First of all, if you have dealt with infertility or know someone who has, you probably have realized that it is unfair. There are many circumstances in life that seem unfair. In the story of Jacob and his brother Esau, there was a blessing to be obtained. This blessing was reserved for the eldest son, in this case Esau. However, God had stated that Jacob, the younger, was to rule over the elder. He was to receive the blessing instead. (Genesis 25:23) As Jacob grew old and was going to die, he took it upon himself to give the blessing to Esau though he knew God's command. Rebekah, their mother, favored Jacob and deceived her husband into giving him the blessing God had promised. Esau returns from hunting to discover this and in verse 34 of Genesis chapter 27 it says: *"And when*

*Esau heard the words of his father, he cried with a great and exceeding **bitter** cry, and said unto his father, Bless me, even me also, O my father."* Esau becomes bitter over the situation he finds himself in. The chapter goes on in verse 41 to show the first visible fruit of bitterness in Esau's life. *"And Esau **hated** Jacob because of the blessing wherewith his father blessed him: and Esau said in his <u>heart</u>, The days of mourning for my father are at hand; then will I slay my brother Jacob."* We then see the bitterness move from producing the fruit of hatred in Esau's heart to his desire to kill his brother and into his soul where it allows rebellion to take over: *"And Esau seeing that the daughters of Canaan pleased not Isaac his father; Then went Esau unto Ishmael, and took unto the wives which he had Mahalath the daughter of Ishmael Abraham's son, the sister of Nebajoth, to be his wife."(Genesis 28:8)* At this point Esau let the vine of bitterness creep into his spirit and succumbed to his own desires and thoughts instead of God's. In the end, Esau and Jacob reconciled, but I believe many blessings Esau could have received, despite his circumstances, were lost because of bitterness.

Chapter 21
Submit to God's Will: God as a Road Map

"But Jonah rose up to flee unto Tarshish from the presence of the Lord..." (Jonah 1:3)

There is a lot of talk about finding the will of God and living in the will of God. This is very important. But perhaps even more so is living *with* the will of God. Many, many people know what God wants them to do. Maybe they have been called to be a missionary or a pastor. A lot of those people resist this and though they have found the will of God, they decided not to live with it. The story of Jonah is a perfect example of this. Jonah knew perfectly well that God wanted him to go and preach to the Ninevites. He thought about how awful those people were and how sorrowful it was that he had to go and be around them. So, he decided to resist the will of God and take matters into his own hands. He ran from God. Resisting a calling of God on your life and fighting against God-ordained circumstances are really no different. God's purpose in our lives is not always our desired plan. But it is always perfect. God has different paths for getting people to different places. Sometimes we have to take the mountainous road and suffer for God as Joseph, Job and Paul did. The path of infertility is not an easy road. Most of our time here is spent in the valleys, trying to find our way to the mountaintop. The road gets rough and rocky, and we resist and **climb** back down. I heard someone say once that if mountains weren't rough, we couldn't climb them. We would just keep **sliding** back down. God takes us on the rocky path because He knows what gets us to the top.

As the Psalmist proclaims *"Teach me thy way, O Lord, and lead me in a plain path because of my enemies."* (Psalm 27:11). We must rely only on God to guide us in the way we should go. Like Jonah God has a specific place for us to go. If we follow His roadmap for our lives, we will be happy with whatever the outcome of our journey through infertility. God's roadmap is His Bible.

Exercising the Fruits of the Spirit Amidst Infertility

I believe that one of the best ways to work through our infertility God's way is to get in touch with what He wants us to produce in our lives. God wants each of us as believers to manifest certain fruits. He expresses this in Galatians 5:22-23. *"But the fruit of the spirit is love, joy, peace, longsuffering, gentleness, goodness, faith, meekness, temperance; against such there is no law."*

If we look at how we act and think each day and ask ourselves what kind of fruit we are producing, we will grow closer to God and finding His plan for our lives. In each fruit of the spirit there are simple ways we can act and react that will show forth God's fruits.

Chapter 22
Love

"By this shall all men know that ye are my disciples, if ye have love one to another." John 13:35

In the book of 1 John, it states that "God is love."(4:8) If we have God living in us then we will certainly have this fruit—right? Well, on some level, yes. However having God's love and exercising it can be two different things. There are two main things God commands us to love and at least one thing God commands us not to love. The first is in Deuteronomy 6:5 *"And thou shalt love the Lord thy God with all thine heart, and with all thy soul and with all thy might."* Second to this God commands us to *"Love thy neighbor as thyself."* (Leviticus 19:18; Matthew 19:19; 22:39; Mark 12:31; Luke 10:27; Romans 13:9; Galatians 5:14; and James 2:8) That is a lot of times to mention one specific command. God says that not only is it important for us to love Him, but also for us to love our 'neighbor.' It can be difficult in the midst of infertility to be around those who have children, especially if they seem 'undeserving' in our minds. But God commands us to love them as we love ourselves. That is a tough command. Just as the kind Samaritan helped the man who was hurt, and just as God helped us in our undeserving state when He sent Jesus to pay the penalty for our sins, we are to love those who bare children no matter how deserving or undeserving they seem. God's command regarding what we are *not* to love can be found in 1 John 2:15: *"Love not the world, neither the things that are in the world. If any man love the world, the love of the Father is not in him."* So if we look at what God considers to be 'in the world' we will find that this includes: *"...the lust of the flesh, and the lust of the eyes, and the pride of life..."* *(I John 2:16)* The question is, where do you place your love? Our families should be important to us, and we should love them. But why do we desire children? Is it to fulfill our lives or to have what the world considers a 'happy' family? God knows exactly what we need to be happy. Perhaps God has pointed out some people that need the love you can give them right now. Think about some people that you would have a hard time loving in the midst of infertility. Not just those that seem to take motherhood for granted, but what about those who say unkind things to you? The Bible says *"A soft answer turneth away wrath; but grievous words stir up anger..."* *(Proverbs 15:1)* How can you prevent your anger from being stirred up? When people question why you are unable to have children, or say rude and unpleasant things to you, how can you answer them softly? The Bible also says *"A gift in secret pacifieth anger..."* *(Proverbs 21:!4)* This is speaking of the anger of the person who gives the gift. Try praying specifically for the people you struggle to love. Maybe make them a simple gift or send them an anonymous note. God will help you love them if you let Him.

Chapter 23
Joy

"...the joy of the LORD is your strength." Nehemiah 8:10

In the middle of infertility there will be days when you feel you just do not have the strength to go on. God says that our strength comes from Him and from having His joy inside of us. If you look up the meaning of joy in the concordance in this passage as well as in the passage on the fruits of the spirit, it means "gladness". If you look up gladness in the dictionary it says several things. I would like to concentrate on two that I found helpful. The first is: "feeling joy or pleasure; delighted; pleased." This can encompass a multitude of things, but the *actual* feeling of joy is involved. It is not easy to fake a joyful attitude successfully. The bible instructs us to "delight thyself in the Lord" (Psalm 37:4) and I believe that this is what is most important about this definition. We need to take our eyes off of our situation and put them on God. If we take the time each day to delight in what the Lord gives us, we can develop this spirit of joy. I recommend something that I tried once during my battle with infertility. Create a notebook or journal for yourself that you carry everywhere with you. Pay attention each day to the beautiful things that are all around you. It may be as simple as a butterfly that unexpectedly lands on your shoulder—or as complex as a meaningful piece of poetry that you found in the back of an old book. As soon as you feel one of those negative feelings well up within you, try to find something nearby that you can delight in. If you ask Him, God will send you just what you need when you need it. Whatever it may be, take the time each day to delight in something that God gives you. The second definition that I found interesting is: "very willing". It appears that gladness also involves a bit of action. Being willing to go through whatever God has for you is important. But how do we do it? Do we tie our ankles to a rope and let God drag us through? Or do we run right along behind God with a smile on our faces. I am not trying to sound like it is a simple task to accomplish, but the spirit of joy involves a cheerful willingness to do the will of God. He will get us through and help us to find that place of completeness in our lives.

Chapter 24
Peace

"And the peace of God, which passeth all understanding shall keep your hearts and minds through Christ Jesus." Philippians 4:7

It is easy to feel as though you are somewhat less than a woman because you are unable to have children. This thought can wreak havoc on your inner peace. God's desire for all of us is to have that "peace of God, which passeth all understanding." (Philippians 4:7) Take comfort, first in the word of God when it states the purpose for mankind: "Thou art worthy, O Lord, to receive glory and honour and power: for thou hast created all things, and for thy pleasure they are and were created." (Revelation 4:11) We were created by God for the primary purpose to glorify, honour and have fellowship with Him. Secondary to that is the purpose of the woman: *"And the LORD God said, It is not good that the man should be alone; I will make him an help meet for him." (Genesis 2:18)* We were designed by God to be the help, or support for our husbands that they would need. 'Meet' means adequate or sufficient. This means that being a family of two is indeed a complete family. There will be hard days when the peace that God offers seems to pass you by. God tells us that in trials we will "come forth as gold" (Job 23:10) There is a certain peace in simply knowing that God is there beside us through those days; but you must acknowledge it to attain it. If you refuse to accept the help that God is offering, you will never realize the peace He wants you to have. Take time each day to pray that God would make you successful in the place you are in your life right now. Not successful by the world's standards, but by God's standards. God will put people in your life to help you along the way. Be careful not to get so distracted by your despair that you miss what God wants you to see. In doing that, you will also miss the peace He has for your life.

Chapter 25
Longsuffering

"...that in me first Jesus Christ might shew forth all longsuffering, for a pattern to them which should hereafter believe on him to life everlasting." 1 Timothy 1:16

This is probably the most necessary and most difficult fruit to manifest in infertility. Patience through hardships that we don't understand are one of life's most heart-wrenching trials. To display longsuffering, or patience in the middle of something that we do not know the outcome of can be challenging. But it does not have to devastate us. Our Saviour was longsuffering in everything that he went through here on earth. We need to work as hard as we can each day to pattern our life after Jesus Christ. To attain that patience through the storm, we need to develop an attitude free from anxiety and full of grace. Prayer is the most powerful way to obtain longsuffering. As you feel the anxiety rise up in you, or the panicky thoughts that plague you, pray and ask God to grant you His grace that you may be longsuffering through your trial. As we develop this fruit, it will become apparent to others around us. Especially in this fast paced society, patience is in short supply. As others see our patience through our trial, they will wonder how to get there too. And as the verse above states so eloquently, we can show forth Christ and his pattern in our lives to "them which should hereafter believe on him..." (1 Timothy 1:16) It can be a wonderful way to witness to those without Christ.

Chapter 26
Gentleness

"...thy gentleness hath made me great." 2 Samuel 22:36

I have always loved the passage that this verse comes from. Just prior to it is the verse, *"He maketh my feet like hinds' feet; and setteth me upon my high places."(vs.34)* The hind, a female deer, is a mountain dweller in some places. Her footing must be stable and firm when traversing over rocky terrain. God wants to do this for us when we go through trials like infertility. The example of the hind is just one of the most beautiful examples of gentleness in nature. She is created perfectly by God and designed to live in the habitat she is born into and the trials that habitat will present. Infertility can present us with so many trials and struggles that it can seem as if we are fighting a battle by ourselves. What is interesting about this verse on gentleness is the word 'great'. It means multiplied. If we strive to manifest God's gentleness, He will multiply us. That may seem an odd statement, but if you really think about it, it makes sense. In our time of battle we need God on our side. When we respond to our situation with gentleness, God gives us the spiritual army we need to fight our battle. So what is gentleness? It may conjure up in your mind images of petting kittens or other things we were taught as a child. This is true, but the spiritual gentleness from God is being able to humble ourselves in the presence of others and God in order to accomplish His will. Just as Christ was afflicted for our sakes, we are to suffer our affliction in gentleness for Him. This may seem simple on the outside, but it is actually very hard. Responding gently, or humbly to the circumstances of infertility can be a challenge. Guarding our responses to other's opinions and recognizing that there are people who just do not, and may never, understand what it is to go through infertility is hard. I found that often when people would make comments in passing to others or in movies, books or yes, even preaching, it was very hard to guard my reaction. My fleshly reaction was one of harshness, anger and defensiveness. I immediately felt that warmth rise up within me, urging me to defend how tender my heart was about what I was going through. I am not saying that we cannot educate others on infertility. They will never truly understand how we feel, but it is okay to let them know how their comment made you feel. The key is gentleness. Recognize their circumstances and remind yourself that they probably have no idea that what they are saying affects you on a personal level. Then, as the Bible says, go to them and make them aware of your circumstance and let them know that you were hurt by their statement. (Matthew 18:15) If they want to know more and you feel comfortable, talk to them. If nothing else, perhaps it will make them more aware of how their words affect others. It is easy to become overly sensitive about being childless. I still feel these feelings when someone is speaking about something that would hurt a person going through infertility. It is a life-changing experience whether you eventually have children or not. Showing forth the fruit of gentleness can help now and in the future.

Chapter 27
Faith

"Now faith is the substance of things hoped for, the evidence of things not seen…" Hebrews 11:1

Did it ever occur to you that you may be the evidence of God to someone else? As in Moses' life, his faith was evident to the Israelites who followed him. The substance of his faith, his actions, showed others that his hope and faith were real. God often must incite action from his children. He does this by allowing certain circumstances in their lives. God does not want us to be 'neutral' Christians. We are in the days when God's preserved Word is our instruction manual on life and our faith in that Word must be shared with those around us in order to bring them to the saving knowledge of Christ. The only way this can happen is through action. Have you ever heard the statement "every action requires an equal and opposite reaction"? How true this is for infertility! If God should allow infertility or any other battle in our lives, it is required that we react to it. How we react to it demonstrates to others how we feel about God. Our faith, the action associated with it, shows those around us the reality of God.

If we react to infertility as though it is a hole in which there is no way out and allow ourselves to succumb to depression and despair, Satan has us right where he wants us. We are useless as a testimony to others of Christ's love and a deflection to those who seek the comfort that only the Holy Spirit can provide. How we react when our faith is tested not only speaks to the lost world around us, but also to other Christians. There may be, perhaps, a young teenager in your church who in a few years will be travelling the same road as you. Maybe they will remember how you reacted when you were going through infertility, or perhaps their parents will remember. Will your pastor have someone he can send them to for counsel and guidance?

Chapter 28
Meekness

"But sanctify the Lord God in your hearts: and be ready always to give an answer to every man that asketh you a reason of the hope that is in you with meekness and fear."
1 Peter 3:15

I have always thought that one of the most unfair statements is "those who cannot do, teach." Teachers are so vital to us in so many ways that to diminish their intelligence or anything else about them seems a great disservice. It takes a meek person to be taught and an even meeker person to teach effectively. The least effective teachers are the ones who think that they know everything and take every chance they have to prove it to everyone else. The most effective teachers are the ones who know that they don't know everything, but take the time to help their students with whatever they are struggling with in a compassionate and patient manner. Meekness is power under subjection. It is knowing the abilities you have within you and acknowledging that they are God-given abilities and using them to serve God instead of self. We have a hope that the lost in this world do not have: the saving grace of God that is manifesting itself within us. Through trials and struggles those without Christ watch us to see if we cling to that hope and wonder how we do it. If we can reign in our selfish thoughts and actions, God will give us the opportunity to share our faith with others. If our life is rosy and happy all the time, those around us will not have a reason to ask about our hope. Just as in the life of Job, Satan said to God, *"Doth Job fear God for nought? Hast not thou made an hedge about him, and about his house and about all that he hath on every side? Thou has blessed the work of his hands, and his substance is increased in the land. But put forth thine hand now, and touch all that he hath, and he will curse thee to thy face."(Job 1:9-11)*

We know from scripture how Job reacted. How will you react?

Chapter 29
Goodness

"My goodness and my fortress; my high tower and my deliverer; my shield and He in whom I trust..." Psalm 144:2

In and of ourselves we have no goodness. Our sprit must yield to His and become new each day in Christ. If we allow Him to be our strength each day and ask him to guide us and work through us, we will be able to show His goodness to others even in difficult circumstances. The verse above states that He is our fortress and our high tower. These are parts of a defensive structure. They offer protection and safety. God offers us these things if we trust in Him. He is also our deliverer, or the soldier who goes to battle for us when we need someone to rescue us from persecution. He is also our shield, with us always to protect us from the weapons of Satan. We must trust in Him for these things. Goodness is listed first here for a reason. If we try to be good in our own strength, we will fail. It is only when we are doing things in His strength that He can offer us the safety and protection of His fortress and high tower. It is only when we submit to Him that we will be delivered. And it is only when we get behind Him that He can be our shield from the wickedness and temptation that this world throws at us. Infertility can present many difficulties in being good to those around us. It may be hard to look the other way when someone makes comments about your infertility. Turning the other cheek takes on a whole new meaning when it comes to a situation as desperately emotional as infertility. The goodness of God was manifested to us when, without sin, Jesus sacrificed himself for us. Even though we give Him every reason not to, He still lovingly gave Himself for us. With God's Spirit in us, we can do the same for those who hurt us so deeply with their words.

Chapter 30
Temperance

"And to knowledge temperance, and to temperance, patience and to patience godliness." 2 Peter 1:6

As a former preschool teacher I can tell you that without a doubt, temperance (or self-control) is the one thing that children struggle with more than anything else. Just about every conflict they have comes from a lack of self-control. Let me say that I prefer to say 'control of self'. It is not that we should be able to control anything we do properly. It is only when we focus on Jesus that we can have a proper Controller in our lives. Poor self control comes from self focus. Preschoolers are very 'me' focused individuals. For the first two years of their life someone has done pretty much everything for them. The world revolves around them. As God's children we are very much the same. If we do not grow and, instead, remain in the self focused preschool years of our Christian life, we will continue to struggle with self control. We can have all the knowledge of a fully grown Christian, but if we do not move forward emotionally and add temperance to that knowledge, we will have a hard time reigning in self focused desires. So how does this apply to infertility? In today's modern medicine and philosophies there are many 'cures' and 'alternatives' offered to us. It would be easy to say that these other options are against God and we should abstain from them. Some of them are. Some of them are not. The hard thing is knowing that many of them may or may not be the avenue God wants us to pursue. We have to take our strong desire to have children and restrain it so we do not focus on our selves when making these important decisions. The verse above also cautions to add to these things patience. Boy do we know about patience. To some this comes easily-others not so much; but we all have to exercise it. Once we focus on God's desire for us and restrain our self focused desires, we can start REALLY exercising patience. Then, we will have accessed the final characteristic in this verse—godliness. A godly individual cannot be one who has no desire for or patience with, God's plan for them. Once thing that I found helpful when struggling with this was to pray for someone else who was going through the same thing as myself. I still prayed for strength to handle what God had for me, but I also prayed for that individual to have strength and for them to receive not only their 'miracle' but also to know what God's plan was for their life.

Salvation

"But Jesus turning unto them said, Daughters of Jerusalem, weep not for me, but weep for yourselves, and for your children. For, behold, the days are coming, in the which they shall say, Blessed are the barren, and the wombs that never bare, and the paps which never gave suck." (Luke 23:28-29)

Can you imagine a time when infertility would be a good thing? No doubt if you have experienced this, you cannot. But God tells us in the above verse that there will come a time when it will be better to be barren than to raise children in this world. Here, Jesus is speaking to the women that followed Him as he went to His death on the cross. He is referring to the coming judgment of God on a nation that has rejected His Son. There is also a coming judgment for those who have not accepted Christ as their Saviour. The Bible tells us that "all have sinned and come short of the glory of God".(Romans 3:23) It also tells us that "the wages of sin is death" This means that what we earn for our sin is death; both physical and spiritual. But God loves us so much that He gave His Son Jesus to pay what we owed for our sin. *"For God so loved the world that he gave his only begotten Son, that whosoever believeth in Him shall not perish but have everlasting life." (John 3:16)* We can know God's forgiveness and have a home in heaven with Him, if we trust in Him as our Saviour. *"I am the way the truth and the life. No man cometh unto the Father, but by me."(John 14:6)* God tells us that if we call upon His Son to save us, we will be saved. *"These things have I written unto you that believe on the name of the Son of God; that ye may know that ye have eternal life..." (1John 5:13)*

There are three simple steps to realizing God's plan of salvation for your life:

A-Admit that you are a sinner.

B-Believe on Jesus Christ as the Son of God to save you.

C-Confess with your mouth in prayer that you believe and accept God's gift of salvation.

If you would like to accept Christ as your personal Saviour, you need to go to Him in prayer, similar to this:

Dear Jesus, I know I am a sinner and that you died and rose from the dead for me. Please forgive me for my sin and take me to heaven when I die. Thank you! Amen.

Afterword
Motherhood after Infertility

Next to overcoming bitterness, perhaps the most challenging place after infertility is the place of motherhood after infertility. Whether you have become a mother through the miracle of adoption or by a miraculous pregnancy, you are not the same as other mothers. Your story is different and it always will be. And that is okay. In that other world where pregnancy is commonplace and sometimes even undesirable, you will stand out. Your heart will tell you every day that there is something different about your life. And there is. God brings us through these things to give us valuable insight and instruction. I wholeheartedly believe this for everyone who has been through it. I am not speaking of a punishment, but of a special and loving message that our gracious heavenly Father wants us to receive and embrace as our own. I cannot speak for your specific lesson, but I believe that God wants everyone who has been through infertility to adhere to 2 Corinthians 1:3-4: *"Blessed be God, even the Father of our LORD Jesus Christ, the Father of mercies, and the God of all comfort; Who comforteth us in all our tribulations, that we may be able to comfort them which are in any trouble, by the comfort wherewith we ourselves are comforted of God."*

You will be sensitive to the struggles of others if you have been through this for any length of time. God will place people in your life for you to help as you have been helped.

Secondly, unless you have a medical issue that guarantees you will be unable to become pregnant, you will always have that wondering question lingering in your heart and mind. *Will I be able to have another child?* You will watch friends have their second, third, maybe fourth children and feel that same strong desire well up in you as it did before. You may even feel guilty for wanting another child. When someone you know takes having children for granted, you will get angry. I believe this is a topic that needs to be addressed and if God allows, I will write a book specifically for these women.

It sounds cliché to say that the end of our story is only the beginning. In fact, it really does not matter what the "end" to my story is. The second half of our struggle with infertility is what you and I make of it. After we accept that this battle is one that God planned for our lives, we can choose to follow God through it, or forge ahead in our own self motivated path. I cannot say what would have happened in my life if I had never had children. I certainly still would be in the daily battle of surrendering my difficulties to God. I will let you in on a secret though. The battle does not end when you have children. In July of 2006 we stepped out on faith and brought a 15 year old girl into our home, sure that this is what God wanted, not so sure we could parent a teenager, (but who really is?) This first month was not without trial, but we just tried to show her that there were people who cared about the choices she made, even if she did not, and people who loved her regardless of those choices. On August 14th or 15th we received a call from our agency telling us that a baby boy had been born and he was ours if we wanted him. This was still foster care, so we knew there was a chance he could go home, as reunification is always the desirable outcome. We went in and talked to the agency and they told us that there was an extreme likelihood that this little boy would be available for adoption after the six months that the state required for foster care was up. We prayerfully considered this and on August 17th we brought home our 6 day old son. We reveled in the first bath and diaper experiences and I enjoyed the late night feedings. About four or five days after he was home, I started to become ill at night. I felt nauseated, as if I had not eaten enough, and eventually my husband was taking over most of the feedings. As the days went on, I realized that I was late. My cycles had always been regular, but occasionally they went on a few days longer, so I gave it a week. My husband bought a cheap test, not wanting to waste money, and we took it. I had never seen two lines before, and so when one was fainter that the other, I had my doubts, but a trip to our doctor confirmed it. We were pregnant! God had blessed us with two miracles. Our daughter was born May 21st, 2007 and so they are 9 months and 10 days apart. I never wanted to perpetuate the myth that if you "just adopt" you will get pregnant. First of all, we had not yet adopted our son. We stepped out on faith in God to take in a child that may be returned to his birth family. Secondly, the statistics on this happening are actually in the 3-5 % range. I always explain to people that it seems so 'common' because no one ever talks about all the people who adopt and never get pregnant just the ones that do because they are so rare.

I praise God for his blessings and miracles. Just prior to our daughter's birth, our teenage foster daughter was moved back with her birth family. We saw her from time to time at church and always had that hope that she would allow God to change her life. Through my experience with her I have learned that the opportunity that God gives is only useful to those who take full advantage of it. Fortunately we have received correspondence from her recently stating that she knew she had made some poor choices and that she wished to grow closer to God and change her life. It is our prayer that she will take this seriously and commit her life to Christ. My husband and I decided to renew our foster care license even though we had been blessed with our two babies. We decided to do so because we knew God had given us many opportunities through having it to get young people into church and see them saved and even grow. In December of 2008 we agreed to do respite for a teenage girl we had previously picked up on our church bus route. When it became evident that the state was not going to allow her to be adopted with her biological brothers, we had a choice to make. In December of 2008 we adopted her. The October before last, we received a call about 24 hour care for an infant girl. Her adoption was just recently finalized. God has many surprises in His will for your life. A dear friend was blessed by this verse and shared it with me.

Psalm 62:5 My soul, wait thou only upon God; for my expectation is from him.

The word "expectation" means "hope". In the

darkness of infertility, a light of hope shines from one to another. You can choose to carry that light or hide in the darkness. God will give you your expectation. It just may not be what you expect.